TRADE PREFERENCES, FOREIGN AID, AND SELF-INTEREST

URI DADUSH

Charleston, SC
www.PalmettoPublishing.com

Trade Preferences, Foreign Aid, and Self-Interest
Copyright by Uri Dadush, 2022
All rights reserved

No portion of this book may be reproduced, stored in a retrieval system, or transmitted in any form by any means–electronic, mechanical, photocopy, recording, or other–except for brief quotations in printed reviews, without prior permission of the author.

Paperback ISBN: 979-8-88590-500-8
eBook ISBN: 979-8-8229-0057-8

TABLE OF CONTENTS

About the Author and This Book   v

CHAPTER 1: TRADE PREFERENCES AND FOREIGN AID   1

1.1. Introduction   1
1.2. A Brief Review of the Literature   3
1.3. Main Results   9

CHAPTER 2: A DYNAMIC THEORY OF INTERNATIONAL TRANSFERS AND OPTIMAL TRADE RESTRICTIONS   16

2.1. Introduction   16
2.2. The Model   17
2.3. First Order Conditions for an Optimum, and the Optimal Tariff   19
2.4. Digression: An Efficiency Approach   25
2.5. A New Transfer Criterion   26
2.6. Analytical Solution of a Special Case of Trade Biased Growth   27
2.7. Summary and Conclusions   40

CHAPTER 3: A DYNAMIC THEORY OF THE OPTIMAL FOREIGN INVESTMENT RESTRICTION   42

3.1. Introduction   42
3.2. Derivation of the "Static" Optimal Tax   43
3.3. Derivation of the Optimal Dynamic Foreign Investment Tax   44

3.4. Analytical Solution of a Special Case of Complementarity   49
3.5. Summary and Conclusion   69
Appendix: Some Suggestive Results Obtained from
Computer Simulations   71

CHAPTER 4: THE OPTIMAL RETALIATION POLICY FOR A SMALL COUNTRY   **75**

4.1. Introduction   75
4.2. The Possibility of an Extreme Threat   76
4.3. The Problem of Credibility   77
4.4. The Possibility of a Moderate Threat   78
4.5. The Effect of the Threat of Retaliation on the Large Country's Policy   79
4.6. Summary and Conclusions   85

Acknowledgements   *87*

ABOUT THE AUTHOR AND THIS BOOK

Uri Dadush is a Research Professor at the School of Public Policy at the University of Maryland. He was Director of the International Trade Department at the World Bank. This book establishes precise conditions for the provision of foreign aid in a nation's self-interest. It is based on the author's Ph.D. dissertation at Harvard, whose original title is "Interdependence in the Growth Process and International Economic Policy".

Dadush's other books include "WTO Accessions and Trade Multilateralism" (with Chiedu Osakwe, co-editor), "Juggernaut: How Emerging Markets Are Transforming Globalization" (with William Shaw), "Inequality in America" (with Kemal Dervis and others), "Currency Wars" (with Vera Eidelman, co-editor) and "Paradigm Lost: The Euro in Crisis".

CHAPTER 1

Trade Preferences and Foreign Aid

1.1. INTRODUCTION

According to the World Bank, in 2020, poor countries received almost 200 billion $ in foreign aid, and total concessional lending to them by the largest multilateral development banks reached $131 billion from $90 billion in 2019. Poor countries also receive preferential treatment in the World Trade Organization. For example, advanced countries, and many large middle-income developing countries such as China and Brazil, grant the Least Developed Countries duty- and quota-free access to their markets across the most exports.

It is believed that aid to poor countries in the form of grants, loans, and trade preferences is the "right thing to do", and this consensus is espoused by legislatures across the more advanced economies that vote their support. But a hardnosed finance minister of a developed country might ask: is it in our *economic self-interest* to grant these preferences and aid? And under what conditions? The surprising fact is that economists have rarely, if at all, addressed these important questions, at least in a formal sense. The main purpose of the neoclassical two-country growth models which comprise this book is to provide a formal answer to the finance minister's questions. In so doing, the book builds upon, and contributes to, three strands of literature in the pure theory of international economics:

- The optimal tariff
- The optimal foreign investment tax
- International Transfers and the Transfer Problem

The central message of the models is that it is in the self-interest of the advanced country to see the developing country grow only insofar as the latter tends to trade more as its income rises (i.e., the developing country's growth is pro-trade biased). This means that the comparative advantage of the developing country remains in the direction of buying more of what the rich country sells and producing what the rich country wants to buy. When that assumption holds it is in the interest of the advanced country (assuming it is large and can affect tis terms of trade) to lower its tariffs below that which is optimal in the short-run, and, similarly, to lower its investment tax on foreign investment, which could become a subsidy. It is also in the interest of the advanced country to grant some amount of aid to the developing country. These various forms of preferential treatment tend to be more "profitable" for the advanced country early in the developing country's growth path and to decline as the developing country matures and reaches a steady state. Another way of stating this conclusion is that investment in the developing country's progress pays the highest dividends early on – there are declining marginal returns in this kid of help, not only in any one period but also over time.

Though we attempt quantification of these results in a computable model, rigorous empirical testing of our theory lies beyond our scope here. Still, it is quite evident that the volume of trade is positively correlated with output, and – often with per capita income as well. Indeed, across the world, trade grew much faster than output prior to the global financial crisis and still keeps pace nowadays. It is also evident, that, as they grow, developing countries tend to develop a middle class and to demand more of the branded and technologically advanced goods and services that advanced countries produce, and that as productivity improves, developing countries also tend to produce more of the raw materials and labor-intensive goods that advanced countries need. These casual observations provide a prima facie justification for aid and preferential treatment in various forms as suggested by the models in this book. Moreover, we observe that some especially successful present or former developing countries – such as China and the Republic of Korea – tend to eventually become competitors of advanced countries, producing more of the goods advanced countries export. Accordingly, the models in this book provide a formal justification for ceasing aid to them, i.e., for the graduation process such as that envisaged by the World Bank.

The rest of this introductory chapter briefly reviews the literature on the topic and goes on to elaborate on the main results of the models in a non-technical fashion.

1.2. A BRIEF REVIEW OF THE LITERATURE

a. The Optimal Tariff

The literature on the Optimal Tariff probably originates with John Stuart Mill (1917 edition of *The Principles*) who suggested that a large country might be able to improve its terms of trade, hence its welfare, by restricting its foreign trade and exploiting its monopoly power. This assertion was later formalized by Bickerdike (1906) and Edgeworth (1908) in a series of contributions in the *Economic Journal*. The proposition that a large country could by levying a tariff improve its welfare relative to the free trade level has never been seriously challenged since—indeed it has, with time, acquired a certain luster as a major theoretically defensible departure from free trade policy.

The optimal tariff proposition was probably the first rigorously established proposition of the theory of protection, and, as such, has provided a building block for several important subsequent contributions. Most of these, however, fall outside the main focus of the book.

An important contribution relevant to our topic is Ryder's (1967) extension of optimal tariff theory to a dynamic, multiperiod framework. Ryder applies a Ramsey optimal growth framework to an Uzawa (1961–62) two sector growth model of a trading country which faces a less than infinitely elastic foreign offer curve. The home country's control variables are, first, the proportion of income which is saved and, second, the terms of trade which are controlled implicitly by adjustment of the level of imports. Ryder explores the conditions for convergence to the steady state and the economy's path through various zones of specialization. He obtains an optimal tariff formula which is identical to the Mill-Bickerdike-Edgeworth "static" result. This is not, of course, to say that the optimal tariff remains unaltered in the course of the growth process—the tariff will vary as the structure (capital-intensity) of the home economy changes. But Ryder's analysis does imply that a "myopic" policy maker preoccupied only by the current period will automatically adopt the tariff that is optimal in the long run.

Since a substantial part of this book is devoted to highlighting the distinction between statically and dynamically optimal policies, it is important to understand the reason for Ryder's result. By assuming that the foreign offer curve is a function only of the current terms of trade, Ryder in effect imposes the assumption that the home country's trade opportunities are *temporally independent*, or that the home country's policies in one period will not affect its trade opportunities (the locus of the foreign offer curve) in the future. It is not surprising, therefore, that it is in the interest of the home country to act as a statically optimizing monopolist, maximizing current gains in every period. The existence of temporally *dependent* opportunities for trade (and investment) are clearly at the heart of the question posed by the imaginary minister of the previous section, and this is in fact the key change in assumptions that explains most of the difference between the theory developed here and that which has gone before. Specifically, we shall show in Chapter 2 that when the foreign country's offer curve is a function not only of the current terms of trade, but also (as is more reasonable) of the foreign capital stock, that the home country's statically optimal policy proves suboptimal in the long run, since such a policy ignores the effect of the tariff on the foreign country's rate of growth, hence on the home country's trade opportunities in the future. This point is further elaborated upon in Section 3 of this chapter.

Departing from our neoclassical framework, the development of models of imperfect competition in the Krugman tradition led recently to a small number of studies that explore the optimal tariff in growth models. These models have shown how the optimal tariff of static models can be modified to be higher or lower, reflecting its effects on R and D investment, the number of new entrants, product variety, etc. (Helpman. 1990; Nalto and Ohdoi, 2009; Bbeladi et al. 2021)

b. The Optimal Foreign Investment Tax

The problem of the optimal foreign investment (or borrowing) tax is in some ways analogous to the problem of the optimal tariff. The basic proposition of the investment tax literature is that a large lending country could profit from levying a tax designed to restrict its competitively determined foreign investment, equating its average and marginal rate of return. Both the optimal tariff and the optimal foreign investment tax are thus designed to exploit monopoly power in international markets. However, the different nature of the empirical problem, which is being tackled, and the very different structure of the models required to study the two phenomena, have induced these two strands of literature to be developed virtually independently.

In fact, it was only in 1960, over half a century after the Bickerdike-Edgeworth contributions, that the first articles on the optimal foreign investment tax appeared. McDougall and Jasay wrote independently to demonstrate the basic proposition outlined above. They found that the optimal tax equals the elasticity of the foreign rate of return with respect to foreign investment. Kemp (1962) complemented the result by showing that a large *borrowing* country also restricts its borrowing at the optimum.

Since then, several authors have made important refinements to this result, but most will be mentioned only briefly since their contributions are peripheral to the object of the thesis. Kemp (1966) and Pearce and Rowan (1966) made the important observation that a large trading country which has sizable foreign investment (or borrowing) needs to account for the interaction between the investment tax and the tariff in determining its optimal policy. In the usual Hecksher-Ohlin model the interaction is the result of the one-to-one relation between factor returns and commodity prices (Stolper and Samuelson (1941)). Both the investment tax and the tariff can be shown to take any sign at the optimum. For example: an investment tax may be a subsidy at the optimum because the outflow of capital causes increased production of the home country's import commodity in the foreign country and this benefit outweighs the monopoly gains obtainable by restricting foreign investment. In the same vein Jones (1964) suggested that analyzing the optimal tax-tariff policy in the usual $2 \times 2 \times 2$ Hecksher-Ohlin model is inappropriate since there is a negligible probability that an equilibrium exists without at least one of the two countries specializing. This objection was circumvented by Gehrels (1971) who obtained the Kemp-Rowan and Pearce results within the framework of a 3 factor $\times$ 2 goods $\times$ 2 countries model. In this thesis the problem of the optimal tariff and of the optimal foreign investment tax are treated independently, and all our results are subject to the important qualification outlined above.

Two contributions which have direct bearing on the results of the book, and which closely parallel the developments in the optimal tariff literature are, first, Hamada's treatment of retaliation within the context of a model of international investment and, second, Bardhan's treatment of the optimal foreign borrowing tax in the context of a dynamic model in which a large country faces a less than infinitely elastic supply of funds.

Hamada's treatment of retaliation is subject to the same criticism as Johnson's treatment of tariffs and retaliation, since Hamada, too, assumes a Cournot type reaction process. One consequence of this assumption is the prediction that a small country will always lose a tariff or tax war. In Chapter 4 we qualify this result under a more general reaction scheme in which the small country can threaten the large country. It will be shown that, at the limit, the small country can induce the large country to revert to a free trade (or free investment) policy.

Bardhan's treatment of the optimal level of borrowing for a large growing country is subject to the same criticism as Ryder's dynamic model of the optimal trade restriction. Specifically, Bardhan assumes that the large country's borrowing opportunities are "temporally independent" in the same way that Ryder assumed temporal independence of trade opportunities. Bardhan, too, concluded that the statically derived prescription remains unaffected in a dynamic world. Chapter 3 demonstrates that when a large investing country faces a less than infinitely elastic demand for funds which contains the foreign capital stock as an argument, Bardhan's result is no longer true.

c. The Transfer Problem

The main question addressed in the literature on the Transfer Problem is whether international transfer of purchasing power will cause the terms of trade of the transferring country to improve or worsen. In the latter case, the transferring country is said to suffer a "secondary burden" over and above the initial cost of the gift. The issue of the existence of a "secondary burden" is not only analytically interesting, but empirically important in view of occurrences such as German Reparations in the wake of World War I, the Marshall Plan of the 1950's, and modern-day aid to the LDC's.

It was, in fact, the problem of German Reparations which prompted the exchange between J.M. Keynes and B. Ohlin in the *Economic Journal* of 1929, in which Ohlin convincingly argued against the "orthodox" view (represented for the occasion by Keynes) that a transferring country would inevitably be afflicted by a secondary burden. Ohlin took an agnostic view instead and argued that the orthodox conviction stemmed from the tendency to ignore the fact that a transfer implies movement of the offer curves of both countries as well as movements along the curves. Viner (1949) was later to acknowledge the orthodox error. Meanwhile Pigou (1932) derived the obvious-once-stated condition that a secondary burden would exist if and only if the sum of the marginal propensities to import is greater than one. This condition has become known as the "transfer criterion".

In recent years much effort has been devoted, rather fruitlessly, to establishing whether there exists a "presumption" that a secondary burden does in fact exist. I tend to agree with the view of some economists (Bhagwati, 1965) that the issue of presumption is probably not a meaningful question in the absence of corroborating empirical evidence. Be that as it may, in the course of a long debate some results have emerged which are worth mentioning. One result is Samuelson's (1968) adaptation of the transfer criterion to account for the existence of transport costs and tariffs (in either case the sum of the marginal propensities to import must be compared to a value greater than 1, assuming that tariff proceeds are redistributed and that transport costs are incurred at least partly in terms of the transferer's export good). Another well-known important result (see for example Takayama, 1972) is that, provided the international equilibrium is stable, a transferring country can never actually gain by effecting a gift.

Transfer theory can be easily extended to consider the effects of a gift of a quantity of a factor of production, such as capital, on the terms of trade. Unlike the case of "purchasing power" transfers where only demand considerations are relevant, the transfer of factors of production requires consideration of the effect on world supply conditions. In such a case, the transfer criterion is still that the sum of the marginal propensities to import must exceed unity, except that the word "propensities" now refers to the derivative of imports with respect to the capital stock (or whatever the transferred factor happens to be) rather than with respect to "purchasing power". This more general formulation accounts for changes in supply conditions. If, for example, "each country puts new resources into the commodity in which it possesses a comparative advantage, such a transfer of resources must improve the terms of trade of the transferer" provided taste patterns in the two countries are similar (Caves and Jones, 1973, p. 462).

In Chapter 2 we shall extend the theory of transfers of resources to a dynamic, multiperiod setting. Specifically, we derive a criterion which determines whether the transfer of a unit of capital induces a "secondary burden" upon the transferring country, accounting not only for current period effects but for future effects as well. Our definition of the term "secondary burden", however, differs from the static model definition. In static models a "secondary burden" is said to exist if the current terms of trade turn against the transferring country. In the multiperiod model of Chapter 2 such a definition would have little meaning since in order to trace the effect of the transfer on the transferring country's welfare we need to account for *future* effects on the terms of trade as well. The approach adopted is to define a "shadow price" in the transferring country's infinite horizon program for both the transferring and receiving country's capital stocks. The "immediate" cost of the transfer is defined to be simply the shadow price of the home capital stock (y); the "total" cost of the transfer is defined to be

$$y - y^*$$

where y^* is the shadow price of the receiving country's capital stock. We then say that there exists a "secondary burden" if and only if $y^* < 0$, an exogenous increase in the foreign country's capital stock decreases the value of the transferring country's program. Using this definition, the condition for the existence of a secondary burden is investigated.

d. Retaliation and cooperation

In Harry Johnson's classic analysis of optimal tariffs and retaliation (1953–54). Johnson assumed a Cournot-type reaction process in which each country in turn sets its optimal tariff taking the other country's policy as given. He demonstrated that, under this reaction scheme, there can exist equilibria where a country gains from an optimal tariff in spite of retaliation. This was an important result, not only because it disproved a widely held belief, but also because it represented the first rigorous attempt to fill what is obviously a lacuna in the theory of protection. Unfortunately, Johnson's has remained an isolated contribution in an area where it is particularly difficult to obtain meaningful results. For the most part, this book is no exception to the vast literature on the subject and assumes away the possibility of retaliation. In Chapter 4 I have, within a very simple framework, tried to come to grips with what I believe is a basic shortcoming of Johnson's Cournot type reaction scheme—the assumption that in setting an optimal tariff each country in turn takes the other's policy as given; I show that, when one country can threaten the other, and the threat is believed, the outcome of the tariff war can be qualitatively different from that induced by a Cournot scheme.

1.3. MAIN RESULTS

a. Premise

In view of the rather technical nature of the ensuing discussion it seems appropriate to describe the nature of the principal results of the thesis in an informal manner. The purpose here is to expose the reader to the structure of the main models, highlighting the essential characteristic which distinguishes it from the structure of traditional models, and providing an intuitive explanation of how this difference in structure implies a different optimal policy. This will be done at some length for the trade model of Chapter 2 (subsection b), and more briefly for the investment model of Chapter 3 (subsection c). Because the only results which are instrumental to the understanding of most subsequent developments relate to the optimal tariff and to the optimal investment tax, I have focused on these. The other principal results will be listed briefly in subsection C.

b. The Optimal Dynamic Tariff (Sections 2.1 to 2.5)

We assume a world in which there are only two countries, both growing and both producing a capital and a consumption good which are traded. For simplicity, we assume no population growth. The first country (home) is assumed to decide on an optimal growth path (which maximises an infinite sum of discounted utilities) and to steer its development by appropriately controlling its rate of capital accumulation (savings) and the volume of its trade with the second (foreign) country—since the home country is assumed to have some monopoly power on the world market, it implicitly controls its terms of trade by way of controlling its volume of trade. The foreign country, on the other hand, is assumed to be "passive" in two respects: first, its rate of capital accumulation is given by some exogenously determined savings fule; second, it is assumed not to retaliate against the home country's trade restrictions. A crucial element in the model is the form of the foreign country's savings rule. It is assumed to be given by

$$S^* = S^*(K^*, P) \qquad S^*_{K^*} > 0, \qquad S^*_P < 0$$

where S^* denotes foreign savings, K^* the foreign capital stock, and P is the world price of capital goods in terms of consumption goods; it is assumed that the home country exports capital goods, so that P represents the terms of trade of the home country. This last assumption justifies the assumption $S^*_P < 0$, the derivative of foreign country savings with respect to the home country's terms of trade is negative, because of the adverse effect of the rise in P on the foreign country's level of real income.

Another crucial relation is the form of the foreign country's "offer function", its excess demand for capital goods (M). It is given by

$$M = M(P, K^*) \qquad M_P < 0, \qquad M_{K^*} \gtreqless 0.$$

Note that the derivative of M with respect to K^* can take any sign. We shall say that the foreign country's growth is "trade biased" ("anti-trade biased") if and only if $M_{K^*} > 0$ ($M_{K^*} < 0$). If $M_{K^*} = 0$, we shall say that the foreign country's growth is "neutral". As we shall see, the degree of trade bias of the foreign country's growth is the central characteristic which determines the results obtained in the trade model.

Consider now the problem of the home country, personified in "the policy maker", regarding the decision on the optimal trade restriction.

A more severe trade restriction implies improved terms of trade (since $M_P < 0$) in the current period, but it also implies a lower rate of capital accumulation in the foreign country (since $S_P^{\cdot} < 0$) which in turn implies a lower foreign capital stock in future periods. If $M_{K^{\cdot}} = 0$ always (as in Ryder (1967)) then the current policy will have no repercussions in the future, and it is clearly in the interest of the policy maker to adopt a policy which maximises his current income at every moment. In this case, there is no difference between the optimal tariff of static models and the dynamically optimal tariff. Consider, next, the case where $M_{K^{\cdot}} < 0$ always, i.e., the foreign country's growth is anti-trade biased always. In this case the fall in the future foreign capital stock implied by the current trade restriction induces a rise in the foreign country's excess demand for imports in the future, and consequently improved terms of trade for the home country. In this case it is clear that the optimal tariff will, at every moment, be greater than the optimal tariff of static models. In analogous fashion it is possible to establish that, if $M_{K^{\cdot}} > 0$ always, i.e., the foreign country's growth is trade biased, the optimal tariff will, at every moment, be smaller than the optimal tariff of static models.

c. The Optimal Dynamic Foreign Investment Tax (Sections 3.1 to 3.4)

Although the structure of the model of international investment is completely different from that of the model of international trade, the underlying reason for the disparity between the results of this thesis and that of the traditional literature is essentially the same. Consequently, we can be considerably briefer in our exposition of the nature of the results.

In the model of international investment both countries grow, and the foreign country is "passive" in the sense of the previous section. Unlike the trade model, only one good is produced by both countries, there is no trade, and the home country is assumed to invest abroad. The good produced by both countries can be employed, in the fashion of Solow (1956) and many others, both as a consumption and (after a costless "transformation" process) as a capital good. We assume that although the consumption good in both countries is identical, the capital good which is obtained in each country by the costless transformation process *may* be different because of differences in knowledge.

Let us focus again on the relations $S^*(\cdot)$ which denotes as before the foreign savings function. In this model

$$S^* = S^*(K^*, K_F) \qquad S^*_{K^*} > 0, \qquad S^*_{K_F} > 0$$

where K^* denotes as before the foreign capital stock, and K_F denotes the stock of the home country's foreign invested capital (henceforth referred to as "foreign investment"). Note that $S^*_{K_F} > 0$; though this is a plausible assumption, it is by no means unassailable, and it is relaxed in the more complete treatment of Chapter 3.

The other key relation in the foreign investment model is the rate of return on foreign investment function r,

$$r = r(K^*, K_F) \qquad r_{K^*} \gtrless 0, \qquad r_{K_F} < 0.$$

Note that r_{K^*}, the effect of an increase in the foreign capital stock on the rate of return on foreign investment can take any sign. Using a definition familiar in price theory, we shall say that K^* and K_F are "complementary" ("competitive" or "substitute") factors if $r_{K^*} > 0$ ($r_{K^*} < 0$). An example of complementary factors is structure and equipment. Examples of substitute factors are any two identical pieces of equipment.

Using a line of argument similar to that developed in the previous section, it is clear that if $r_{K^*} = 0$ always, the factors are independent, the optimal investment restriction accounts only for current effects and the optimal investment tax is identical to that of static models. This we shall call the "Bardhan" (1967) case. If, on the other hand, the factors are complementary, today's investment restriction, which always causes a fall in the future K^* (since $S_{K_F} < 0$) will induce a fall in the rate of return available in the future (since $r_{K^*} > 0$). It follows that the optimal investment tax must be lower than that of static models. A similar argument establishes that if the factors are substitutes ($r_{K^*} < 0$), the optimal tax is higher than that of static models.

c. Other Principal Results

The other principal results of the thesis will be briefly listed here for the reader's information:

(i) A new transfer criterion (Section 2.5)
It is shown that, in a multiperiod model, the transferring country will suffer a "secondary burden" only if the foreign country's growth is anti-trade biased.

(ii) The optimal control of an LDC's growth pattern by a developed country: model of trade (Section 2.6)
We demonstrate that when the LDC's growth is trade biased, the optimal control of the LDC's growth requires that it be subsidised at first through lower tariffs or outright gifts, with the level of aid declining as the steady state is approached.

(iii) The optimal control of an LDC's growth pattern by a developed country: model of investment (Section 3.4)
When the LDC's capital stock is complementary to that of the developed country one finds the same control pattern as obtains in subsection (ii) above.

(iv) The effect of a change in the rate of time preference of the developed country on its policy towards the LDC: Models of trade (Section 2.6)
It is shown that a rise in the rate of time preference induces the developed country to adopt a "harsher" trade restriction, implying a fall in the LDC's steady state capital stock.

(v) The magnitude of dynamic effects in a neoclassical framework: Model of investment (Appendix to Chapter 3)
Computer simulations indicate that the change in the statically optimal investment tax required by dynamic considerations is often of significant magnitude, but never dominant. By way of contrast, it is shown that it is possible for a developed country actually to *gain* by transferring a unit of capital to a less developed country.

(vi) The optimal retaliation policy for a small country: Static model of investment (Chapter 4)
We demonstrate that, in contrast to the results of Cournot reaction schemes, a small country can, provided the large country believes the small country's threats, induce the large country to adopt a close to free trade policy.

REFERENCES

Bardhan, P. K., "Optimum Foreign Borrowing" in K. Shell, ed., *Essays on the Theory of Optimal Economic Growth*, MIT Press, 1967.

Beladi, H. et al "Optimal Tariffs in a two-country R and D based Growth Model" *Macroeconomic Dynamics*, June 1921

Bhagwati, J., "The Pure Theory of International Trade: A Survey" *in Surveys of Economic Theory*, Macmillan, 1965.

Bickerdike, C. F., "The Theory of Incipient Taxes", *Economic Journal*, December 1906.

Caves, R. E. and R. W. Jones, *World Trade and Payments*, Little, Brown and Co., 1973.

Edgeworth, F. Y., "Appreciations of Mathematical Theories", *Economic Journal*, 1908, pp. 392 and 541.

Gehrels, R., "Optimal Restrictions on Foreign Trade and Investment", *American Economic Review*, LXI, March 1971.

Hamada, K., "Strategic Aspects of Taxation on Foreign Investment Income", *Quarterly Journal of Economics,* August 1966.

Hartman, D., Taxation of Foreign Source Investment Income, Dissertation, Harvard University, 1976.

Helpman, E. "Monopolistic Competition in Trade Theory" Princeton Special Papers, 1990

Jasay, A. E., "The Social Choice Between Home and Overseas Investment", *Economic Journal*, Vol. 70, 1960.

Johnson, H. G., "Optimum Tariffs and Retaliation", *The Review of Economic Studies*, 1953–54.

Jones, R. W., "International Capital Movements and the Theory of Tariffs and Trade", *Quarterly Journal of Economics*, 81, February 1967.

Kemp, M. C., "Foreign Investment and the National Advantage", *Economic Record*, Vol. 38, March 1962.

Kemp, M. C., "The Gain from International Trade and Investment: A Neo-Hecksher-Ohlin Approach", *American Economic Review*, LVI (September 1966).

McDougall, G. D. A., "The Benefits and Costs of Private Investment from Abroad: A Theoretical Approach", *Economic Record*, XXVI, March 1960.

Mill, J. S., *Principles of Political Economy*, Longmans and Green, London, 1917.

Musgrave, P. B., *Direct Investment Abroad and the Multinationals: Effects on the United States Economy*, Senate Foreign Relations Committee Print, 94th Congress, First Session, 1975.

Keynes, J. M., "The German Transfer Problem", *Economic Journal*, March 1923.

Naito, T. and Ohdoi, R. "A two-country model of trade and growth with international knowledge spillovers*" Journal of Economics*, May 2011

Ohlin, B., "The Reparation Problem: A Discussion", *Economic Journal*, June 1929.

Pearce, I. F. and D. C. Rowan, "A Framework for Research into the Real Effects of International Capital Movements" in T. Gagiotti, ed., *Essays in Honor of Marco Fanno*, Cedani, Padova, 1966.

Pigou, A. C., "The Effects of Reparations on the Rates of International Exchanges", *Economic Journal*, December 1932.

Ryder, H., "Optimal Accumulation and Trade in an Open Economy of Moderate Size", in *Essays on the Theory of Optimal Economic Growth,* K. Shell, ed., Cambridge, Massachusetts, MIT Press, 1967.

Samuelson, P. A., "The Transfer Problem and Transport Costs" in *Readings in International Economics*, R. E. Caves and H. G. Johnson, eds., Irwin, 1968.

Solow, R. M., "A Contribution to the Theory of Economic Growth", *The Quarterly Journal of Economics*, February 1956.

Stolper, W. F. and P. A. Samuelson, "Protection and Real Wages", *Review of Economic Studies,* 1941.

Takayama, A., *International Trade,* Holt, Rhinehart and Winston, 1972.

Thurow, L. C. and H. White, "Optimum Trade Restrictions and Their Consequences", *Econometrica,* Vol. 44, July 1976.

Thurow, L. C., "International Factor Movements and the American Distribution of Income", *Intermountain Economic Review,* Vol. II, No. 1, Spring 1976.

Uzawa, H., "On a Two-Sector Model of Economic Growth", *Review of Economic Studies,* 1961–62.

Viner, J., *Studies in the Theory of International Trade,* New York, 1937.

CHAPTER 2

A Dynamic Theory of International Transfers and Optimal Trade Restrictions

2.1. INTRODUCTION

The objective of this chapter is to provide a framework within which two much-investigated topics in international trade theory, the optimal tariff problem and the transfer problem, can be analysed in a dynamic, multi-period setting.

The essential difference between the approach of the paper and the traditional one-period static approach is that in evaluating a tariff policy or a transfer policy, the effect of the home country's action on the foreign country's growth, hence on future terms of trade is accounted for.

This characteristic is also the essential point of departure from analyses, such as that of Ryder (1967), which assume that the home country is optimising over several time periods, but that the foreign offer curve is not a function of the foreign country's capital stock; stated otherwise, Ryder assumes that the home country's trade opportunities are temporally independent.

Whilst Ryder's analysis provided a confirmation of the static result, that the optimal tariff is the reciprocal of the elasticity of the foreign offer curve, our model leads to a general optimal tariff formula which is decomposable into a "static" component (identical to the classic formula) and a "dynamic" component whose sign depends on the degree of trade bias of the foreign country's growth. If the foreign country's growth is trade biased (i.e., the growth elasticity of the foreign offer curve is positive) the dynamic component of the tariff is in fact a subsidy. Otherwise, it is an additional tax.

In the context of the same model a new transfer criterion is defined to measure the "true cost" of an international transfer of one unit of capital at the margin. It is found that the degree of trade bias of the foreign country's growth also determines whether there exists a "secondary burden". If the foreign country's growth is trade biased there will be no secondary burden and the initial cost of a transfer is at least partially recouped.

The plan of the chapter is as follows: in Section 2.2 the structural relations of the general model are presented; in section 2.3 the necessary conditions for an optimum are used to derive an optimal tariff formula; section 2.4 indicates that the optimal tariff formula of section 2.3 may be derived from pure Pareto-efficiency criteria; in section 2.5 a new transfer criterion is defined and the conditions under which a transfer implies a secondary burden are discussed.

In section 2.6 a special case of trade bias is analysed in which the home country is developed, and the foreign country is less developed: the dynamics of the optimal tariff formula and the transfer criterion are explored in detail.

2.2. THE MODEL

The world consists of two trading countries, both producing a capital good and a consumption good. For ease of discussion, and without loss of generality, it is assumed that the home country imports consumption goods. The problem we shall consider is that of the home country's policy maker, who is searching for a tariff-path and a savings stream which maximise a discounted sum of utilities. In so doing the policy maker accounts for the effect of his policy on the foreign country's rate of capital accumulation and its effect on the terms of trade in the future. One direct result of the exercise is a new optimal tariff formula. An important by-product is a new transfer criterion which evaluates the true cost of foreign aid.

The home country's problem is set out as a problem in the calculus variations with two state variables, the home and the foreign capital stock, and two control variables, the terms of trade and the production level of capital goods in the home country. The notation and the problem are set out as follows[1] (time scripts will usually be omitted hereafter):

---

1 Several other equivalent formulations of the problem are possible of course. This was found to be the most convenient.

The Problem

$$\text{Max} \int_0^\infty e^{-\delta t} u(c(t))\, dt$$

subject to …

CONSTRAINT	
(1) $\bar{C}(t) = F(\bar{Q}(t),\ K(t))$	(1) Home Production Possibility frontier
(2) $M(P(t),\ K^*(t)) + \bar{C}(t) = C$	(2) Walras constraint or Balance of Payments constraint
(3) $\dot{K}(t) = \bar{Q} - M(\cdot)/P(t) - \lambda K(t)$	(3) Equation of motion of home capital stock
(4) $\dot{K}^*(t) = S^*(P(t),\ K^*(t)) - \lambda^* K^*(t)$	(4) Equation of motion of foreign capital stock
(5) $K(0) = K_0,\ K^*(0) = K_0^*$	(5) Initial conditions

Notation in order of appearance

$\int_0^\infty L$	:	Welfare functional with infinite horizon
δ	:	Discount factor
$U(C)$	:	Instantaneous utility of consumption
t	:	Time index
$\bar{C}$	:	Production of consumption goods in the home country
$\bar{Q}$	:	Production of capital goods in the home country
K	:	Home capital stock
K^*	:	Foreign capital stock
$F(\cdot)$	:	Production possibility curve, home country
P	:	Terms of trade: price of capital goods in terms of consumption goods
$M(P, K^*)$	:	Foreign country's offer function of consumption goods
$\dot{X}$	:	$\dfrac{dx}{dt}\left(e.g.\ \ \dot{K} = \dfrac{dK}{dt}\right)$
λ	:	Depreciation rate of home capital
λ^*	:	Depreciation rate of foreign capital
$S^*(\cdot)$	:	Foreign gross savings function

Some comments are in order about the structure of the model. First note that both the foreign country's offer function $M(\cdot)$ and the savings function $S^*(\cdot)$ are expressed in very general reduced form, depending only on the current terms of trade and the current foreign capital stock. The savings functions often encountered in growth theory (such as for example the proportional, or the Marxian savings assumptions) are all special cases of our general formulation. Second, note that the foreign country is assumed to be "passive", i.e., it is expected not to retaliate in the face of trade restrictions imposed by the home country—the foreign country is just an amalgamation of competing consumers and producers unwilling or unable to collude. This admittedly unsatisfactory assumption is almost invariably made in static analysis and is only justifiable as a first approach in view of the difficulties inherent in alternative formulations.

Third, note that we have assumed no labour growth in the model and that the home and foreign production functions contain no reference to the fixed factor of production labour. This assumption can easily be relaxed by an appropriate redefinition of units leaving results unaffected *provided* we assume that both the home and foreign technology exhibit constant returns to scale, an assumption we shall not require in what follows.

2.3. FIRST ORDER CONDITIONS FOR AN OPTIMUM, AND THE OPTIMAL TARIFF

a. First order conditions

In this section we shall characterise the solution to the home country's problem by deriving the first order necessary conditions for an optimum. The second order necessary conditions are assumed to hold.[2] For simplicity, we shall restrict our attention to interior solutions only.

---

2 Second order conditions are satisfied given concavity of the Hamiltonian with respect to the control and the state variables—such concavity is normally assured by neoclassical "good-behaviour" assumptions.

In order to derive the F.O.C., we need to define an extended instantaneous utility function H (Hamiltonian in mathematics)

$$H = e^{-\delta t}\{U(F(\bar{Q}, K) + M(P, K^*)\} + Y\left(\bar{Q} - \frac{M(P, K^*)}{P} - \lambda K\right) \\ + Y^*(S^*(K^*, P) - \lambda^* K^*)\} \quad (6)$$

where net investment at home and net investment abroad enters weighted by "shadow prices" Y and Y^* respectively. These shadow prices have an *exact* interpretation as the marginal utility of an extra unit of capital, for example:

$$e^{-\delta t} Y^* = \frac{\partial J}{\partial K^*}$$

where J is the maximised value of the welfare functional.

At any given point in time, the Y's and the K's are given, and a necessary condition for an optimum is that H be maximised with respect to the controls $\bar{Q}$ and P.

Deriving (6) with respect to $\bar{Q}$, and denoting partial derivatives with subscripts, and equating to zero, we obtain:

$$\frac{U_c}{Y} = \frac{1}{-F_{\bar{Q}}} \quad (6a)$$

The marginal rate of substitution between investment and consumption goods equals the domestic rate of transformation[3].

Similarly, the condition on P yields:

$$\frac{U'}{Y} = \frac{1}{P}(1 + 1/\eta) - \frac{Y^*}{Y}\frac{\partial S^*/\partial P}{\partial M/\partial P} \quad (7)$$

where η is the elasticity of the foreign offer curve define positive.

Condition (7) has a familiar interpretation: the domestic rate of substitution between consumption and investment goods must equal the foreign rate of transformation. That the right hand side is indeed the FRT, can

---

3 Clearly investment goods have only an *implicit* marginal utility Y.

CHAPTER 2: OPTIMAL DYNAMIC TRADE RESTRICTION

be better seen by noting that a reduction of one unit of consumption goods imports implies an increase $1/P$ in available investment goods, plus a "terms of trade bonus" $\frac{1}{P}\frac{1}{\eta}$ due to the improvement in the terms of trade because of reduced imports, plus or minus a "foreign growth effect" $\frac{Y^*}{Y}\frac{\delta S^*/\delta P}{\delta M/\delta P}$ due to the effect of reduced trade on the foreign country's growth.

b. The optimal tariff

Equation (7) above can be used directly to obtain a formula for the optimal tariff. Such a tariff may be viewed as an "implicit" tariff if the policy maker decides on a quota of exports or imports, thus avoiding the decentralisation problem, or as an explicit tariff provided that the welfare functional of our problem also has behavioural significance. By this we mean that the behaviour of residents can be represented by that of a single individual (policy maker). In the latter case it is necessary to extend some strong assumptions made in static models to our dynamic world. Specifically, we need to assume that all trading is done in the form of futures contracts at the beginning of the planning period and that futures are devoid of uncertainty. This is an extension of the Walrasian auctioneer concept: the auctioneer announces infinite *price-paths* which are wriggled until equilibrium is reached; only then are contracts signed. Under this scheme it is also necessary to assume that the home country's administrator announce the appropriate tariff path *before* trading takes place.

The optimal tariff path is derived as follows. First note that, in a competitive regime, consumers purchase consumption goods abroad until

$$\frac{U'}{Y} = \frac{1}{P}$$

The rate of substitution is equated to the world price. This contrasts with condition (7) where the "social cost" of purchasing foreign consumption goods differs from the price facing individuals $1/P$. At every moment a tariff θ is needed on imports of consumption goods which equates the individuals' cost to the social cost

$$1/P(1 + \theta) = 1/P(1 + 1/\eta) - \frac{Y^*}{Y}\frac{\partial S^*/\partial P}{\partial M/\partial P}$$

implying

$$\theta = \frac{1}{\eta} - \frac{Y^*}{Y}\frac{\partial S^*/\partial P}{\partial M/\partial P}P$$

Rewriting in terms of elasticities,

$$\theta = \frac{1}{\eta} - \frac{Y^*}{Y}\frac{\eta_{S^*/P}}{\eta}\frac{S^*}{M/P} \qquad (7a)$$

where $\eta_{S^*/P}$ denotes the elasticity of S^* with respect to $P\left(=\frac{\partial S^*}{\partial P}\frac{P}{S^*}\right)$.

The optimal tariff is composed of a "static" component $1/\eta$ which is identical to the optimal tariff of one period models, less a "dynamic" component $\frac{Y^*}{Y}\frac{\eta_{S^*/P}}{\eta}\frac{S^*}{M/P}$.

If we impose the regularity condition $\eta > 0$ (i.e. the foreign country's offer of consumption goods decreases if the world price of consumption goods decreases), the sign of the dynamic component will depend on the sign of y^* and $\eta_{S^*/P}$ (y is positive in view of condition 6a).

Consider first the sign of $\eta_{S^*/P}$. It is well known that a worsening in the terms of trade of a country reduces its level of real income. In what follows we shall assume that foreign savings are positively related to the level of foreign real income, implying $\eta_{S^*/P} > 0$. It is important to realise, however, that this assumption is by no means unassailable. For example, Hecksher-Ohlin type models of trade and growth have been proposed in the past (Bardhan, 1966) where the propensity to save out of capital and labour income differ; if, as assumed here, the foreign country exports consumption goods, and the latter are labour intensive, and the propensity to save out of capital income is higher than that out of labour income, an improvement in the foreign country's terms of trade *could* actually lead to lower foreign savings.

Abstracting from these distributional considerations we have $\eta_{S^*/p} > 0$ and the sign of the dynamic component will depend only on the sign of y^*. If $y^* > 0$, i.e., if an increase in the foreign capital stock increases the value of the home country's program, the sign of the dynamic component is positive, and the optimal tariff is reduced below the statically optimal level.

In the next two sections, the relation between the sign of y^* and the underlying structure of the foreign country's economy is investigated under the assumption of steady state. First, however, we redirect the reader's attention to equation (7a). It is interesting to note that at any point in time the dynamic component is larger, the larger is Y^*, the shadow price of the foreign capital stock; the smaller is Y, the shadow price of the home capital stock; the greater the sensitivity of foreign savings to the terms of trade; the smaller is the price elasticity of the foreign offer curve; the larger is foreign savings with respect to the home country's exports of capital goods. Only when $Y^* = 0$, i.e., when the foreign country's growth has no effect on the home country's program, will the optimal tariff equal the tariff of static models.

c. The optimal tariff in the Steady State

Further insight can be gained into the determinants of the dynamic component by using information contained in other necessary conditions for optimality and imposing the assumption that the system is in a steady state. We shall not, in this very general model attempt to rationalise the assumption of steady state by exploring stability conditions or by demonstrating the "turnpike" property of the system—this will be done under more restrictive assumptions in section 2.6.

Another necessary condition for optimality is given by:

$$\frac{\partial H}{\partial K^*} + (e^{-\delta t} Y^*) = 0$$

which is usually interpreted to mean that the marginal productivity of capital plus "capital gains" must equal zero. This equation is written:

$$\left(\frac{U'}{Y} - \frac{1}{P}\right) \eta_{M/K^*} \frac{M}{K^*} + \frac{Y^*}{Y}\left(\eta_{S^*/K^*} \frac{S^*}{K^*} - \lambda^* - \delta\right) + \frac{Y^*}{Y} = 0$$

where η_{M/K^*} and η_{S^*/K^*} are respectively elasticities of M and S^* with respect to K^*.

In the steady state $\dot{Y}^* = 0$ by definition. Also, by assumption

$$\frac{U'}{Y} - \frac{1}{P} = \frac{1}{P_b} - \frac{1}{P} = \theta \frac{1}{P}$$

Using these conditions, (8) can be rewritten:

$$\frac{Y^*}{Y} = \frac{\theta \eta_{M/K^*} \cdot \frac{M/P}{K^*}}{\delta + \lambda(1 - \eta_{S^*/K^*})} \qquad (9)$$

Substitution (9) into (7) and rearranging, we obtain an expression for the optimal steady state tariff, denoted $\hat{\theta}$:

$$\hat{\theta} = \frac{1}{\eta + \dfrac{\eta_{M/K^*} \cdot \eta_{S^*/P} \lambda}{\delta + \lambda(1 - \eta_{S^*/K^*})}} \qquad (10)$$

where we used the condition that in the steady state $S^* = \lambda^* K^*$ (Gross Savings equals depreciation). The advantage of expression (10) over expression (7) is that we have been able to eliminate the rather inscrutable term Y^*/Y, replacing it by more directly interpretable elasticities.

There are several things to note about expression (10). First, note that even in the steady state the optimal tariff is different from that derived in static models (which is simply $1/\eta$). Second, note that the sign of the "dynamic term" (the second expression in the denominator) depends on the sign of η_{M^*/K^*}, the "growth elasticity" of the foreign country's exports, a direct measure of trade bias.

Expression (10) leads directly to our first principal conclusion. First, note that, even in the steady state the optimal tariff is different from that derived in static models (which is simply $1/\eta$). Second, note that we can safely assume $\eta_{S^*/K^*} < 1$, since otherwise the foreign country's steady state equilibrium would not be stable in isolation (see Samuelson's discussion of this condition, 1965). Consequently, we have

In the steady state the optimal tariff is lower than the statically optimal tariff if and only if $\eta_{M^*/K^*} > 0$, the foreign country's growth is trade biased.

Note finally that provided we can assume that the elasticities are approximately constant, we can say that the higher the rate of time preference δ, the smaller the importance of dynamic effects, an expected result.

2.4. DIGRESSION: AN EFFICIENCY APPROACH

The purpose of this section is to demonstrate that the formula for the optimal tariff can be derived using a pure efficiency, or Pareto-Optimum criterion, rather than an explicit welfare function.[4]

It is a well known theorem of welfare economics that given a convex opportunity set, an allocation C belonging to the opportunity set is Pareto-Optimal if and only if it maximises a function $Y'C$ for some $\gamma \leq 0$ (γ is usually interpreted as a price vector). Applying this result to our problem, we can say that if a consumption path is Pareto-Optimal, then it must solve:

$$Max \int_0^\infty \gamma(t) C(t)\, dt$$

subject to conditions (1) through (5) for some $\{\gamma(t)\} \geq 0 (\neq 0)$.

It is simple to verify that in order for a consumption path to be optimal, precisely the same necessary conditions hold as were discussed in section 2.3, except that the parameter δ is replaced by the expression $\dot{\gamma}(t)/\gamma(t)$, the

---

[4] It is not surprising that this should be possible, since in static models the optimal tariff can be derived by equating FRT and DRT (the slopes of the foreign offer curve and the home production possibility curve) without reference to indifference surfaces.

instantaneous rate of change of the weights $\{\gamma(t)\}$, and the marginal utility $U_C(C(t))$ is replaced by the weight $\gamma(t)$. Moreover, the optimal tariff formula is precisely the same as 7(a) obtained from maximising the explicit welfare functional.

What this argument amounts to is that unless the optimal tariff policy of section (3) is adopted, it is always possible to find a consumption path which increases consumption in at least one period, without decreasing it in any other period.

2.5. A NEW TRANSFER CRITERION

What is the true cost to the home country of giving away one unit of capital as "foreign aid"? At the margin, foregoing one unit of capital implies a welfare loss Y, the shadow price of K. This loss, however, will be offset (or amplified) by the quantum Y^*, which reflects the effect of increasing the foreign country's capital endowment K^*. Thus, the net loss (or gain?) may be expressed simply as $Y - Y^*$, or, in a unit free expression as:

$$t = \frac{Y - Y^*}{Y} = 1 - \frac{Y^*}{Y}$$

where t denotes the "transfer criterion" and is to be interpreted as the proportion of the immediate cost of the transfer which is recouped. We shall say that the transfer is "at more than cost" if $t > 1$, "at full cost" if $t = 1$, "at less than cost" if $t < 1$, "at gain" if $t < 0$.

The true cost of a transfer will depend on the sign of Y^*/Y, which, intuition suggests, will depend on the degree of trade bias of the foreign country's growth. This is confirmed by inspecting the expression for the steady state value of Y^*/Y (equation reproduced below).

$$\frac{Y^*}{Y} = \frac{\theta \eta_{M/K^*} \cdot \frac{M/P}{K^*}}{\delta + \lambda(1 - \eta_{S/K^*})} \qquad (10a)$$

Assuming that $\theta > 0$ (i.e., that the foreign country's growth is anti-trade biased, or that it is trade-biased but not sufficiently so to make the steady state tariff a subsidy) and, as before, that $\eta_{S^*/K^*} < 1$, we have:

$$\operatorname{sgn} \frac{Y^*}{Y} = \operatorname{sgn} \eta_{M/K^*}$$

Thus our second principal conclusion emerges, that *in the steady state, given some "regularity conditions", the transfer will be at less than cost* $(t < 1)$ *if and only if the foreign country's growth is trade biased* $(\eta_{M/K^*} > 0)$.

Note, moreover, that at any point in time the proportion of the transfer that is recouped, Y^*/Y, will be higher the greater the proportion of capital exports to the total foreign capital stock $\left(\dfrac{M/P}{K^*}-\right)$, the lower are foreign production cost in relation to home production costs (θ), and the lower the rate of time preference, and the higher the degree of trade bias of the foreign country's growth.

2.6. ANALYTICAL SOLUTION OF A SPECIAL CASE OF TRADE BIASED GROWTH

a. Premise

In this section we shall analyse in detail a special case of the general model presented above. The model we shall now present is intended to depict a situation where a developed country (DC), producing a "technologically sophisticated" capital good and a consumption good, trades with a less developed country (LDC) which produces only consumption goods, and whose growth is trade biased.

The most important restriction imposed in the model below is that the home country's capital stock is constrained to be constant, and only the foreign LDC country is allowed to grow. This assumption permits us to "exogenise" one control variable ($\bar{Q}$), one state variable (K), and the related shadow price (Y) and to enormously simplify the characterisation of the optimal path. An assumption of this type is essential if we are to use phase diagrams in order to analyse the dynamics of the system, a technique which can obviously only be applied to track only two, or, at most, three variables. It is hoped that the qualitative results would not differ substantively from those of a model in which the DC may grow but is close to a steady state situation.[5]

b. The Model

In this and the following sections we shall employ the same notation as in the preceding discussion, with starred variables referring to the LDC and plain variables referring to the DC.

The DC's utility is assumed linear:

$$U(C) = C$$

and its technology is assumed to be a neo classical, well-behaved production possibilities function:

$$\bar{C} = \Phi(\bar{Q}, K_0) \qquad \Phi' < 0, \quad \Phi'' < 0$$

where K_0 is the capital endowment of the home country, which as already indicated is restricted to a stationary state. For convenience, and without affecting any of our results, we shall assume that DC capital does not depreciate.

The LDC is assumed to be completely specialised in the production of consumption goods:

$$\bar{C}^* = \Phi^*(K^*)$$

with $\Phi^{*\prime} \equiv r > 0, \qquad \Phi^{*\prime\prime} < 0$

where r denotes the marginal productivity of capital in the foreign country.

---

5 This phenomenon was in fact experienced in the computer simulation of a model of similar mathematical structure; see the appendix to Chapter 3.

The LDC's demand for imports of capital goods (offer of consumption goods expressed in terms of capital goods) is in this model identical to the savings function, denoted S^*. It is assumed of the "separable" form:

$$S^*(K^*, P) = \Phi^*(K^*)/F(P)$$

where

$$F' > 0, \quad F'' > 0.$$

This form is consistent, for example, with a C.E.S. utility function defined over capital and consumption goods. It can perhaps best be interpreted as a proportional savings function, with the proportion of income saved depending on the price of capital goods. The assumption $F'' > 0$ is a second-order requirement, which, in the case of C.E.S., implies that the elasticity of the foreign offer curve is greater than one, a standard condition.

The condition $\Phi^{*\prime} > 0$ ensures that the foreign country's growth is trade biased, since an increase in the foreign capital stock at constant terms of trade implies an increase in the foreign offer of consumption goods.

We can now write the DC's problem in full (time subscripts are omitted):

$$Max \int_0^\infty e^{-\delta t} c \, dt$$

Subject to

CONSTRAINT	DESCRIPTIONS
(11) $C = \Phi(\bar{Q}, K_0) + P\bar{Q}$	(11) DC's Walras constraint or Balance of Payments constraint
(12) $\bar{Q} = \dfrac{\Phi^*(K^*)}{F(P)}$	(12) Equilibrium in world markets
(13) $\dot{K}^* = \bar{Q} - \lambda K^*$	(13) Motion of LDC capital stock
(14) $K^*(0) = K_0^*$	(14) Initial condition

The only control variable of this problem is P (the variable $\bar{Q}$ can be eliminated using condition (12)), and the only state variable is K^*.

Since our main interest here is not the study of patterns of specialisation and consequent corner solutions, we shall avoid the problem by assuming:

$$-\Phi'(0, K) = 0, \qquad -\Phi'(\bar{Q}^K, K) = \infty$$

where $\bar{Q}^K$ is the maximum amount of $\bar{Q}$ which can be produced given a capital stock $\bar{K}$. This assumption ensures that, at any level of the home capital stock, and at any terms of trade, the home country will produce some of both goods.

Recapitulating, the home DC's problem is to manipulate optimally its terms of trade so as to maximise an infinite sum of discounted consumption. The terms of trade are manipulated implicitly by controlling the level of output of capital goods, all of which must be exported by assumption. Note that the assumption $F' > 0$ and the equilibrium relation (12) ensure that to any $\bar{Q}$ there corresponds a unique P. Also note that condition (11) ensures that a unique C corresponds to a given $\bar{Q}$ (hence, to a given P).

In this model, restricting today's exports of capital goods, implies a smaller supply of consumption goods in the future since the LDC's trade-biased growth is stifled. We shall therefore expect an optimal tariff which is lower than the static tariff, and our transfer criterion to indicate that transfers are always at less than cost.

Before we can focus on the optimal path of the tariff and the size of the transfer criterion along the optimal path, we need to characterise the path of the basic variables K^*, Y^*, P.

c. Characterisation of the optimal path

This section applies the standard techniques of stability analysis to demonstrate analytically that the system converges to a steady state from any point in the vicinity of this long run equilibrium. The steady state is shown to be a saddle point equilibrium so that the system exhibits the turnpike property (the link between the saddle point and the turnpike property is brought out in Samuelson, 1965). It will be shown that if, as we assume, the LDC's capital stock is initially below its steady state value, the approach to the steady state is characterised by a steady rise in K^*, fall in Y^*, and rise in P.

It is worthwhile to point out that there is an essential difference between the concept of steady state stability as applied to a normative model of the type we are analysing, and as applied to a positive or descriptive model of the type considered, for example, by Oniki and Uzawa. In the latter model stability analysis attempts to answer the question: "Will the impersonal market mechanism lead to a steady state?"; in our model the question asked is, "Is it desirable for the DC's policy maker to steer the LDC towards a steady state?" Even though the mathematical techniques employed in the analysis of the two problems are identical, the distinction is an important one for two reasons. First, because demonstration of the LDC's steady state stability in our model has a fundamental implication, *that it is in the DC's interest to make the LDC grow until the steady state is reached,* and that it is in the PC's interest to make the LDC contract if the latter happens to be initially above its steady state capital stock. Second, because, as Kurz (1968) has pointed out, the assumption of a policy maker steering the system towards steady state makes the concept of saddle point stability more palatable, since we can rest assured that a random deviation from the unique stable path can always be consciously corrected.

The first step of the demonstration consists in defining the Hamiltonian of the problem and deriving the first order conditions. In the second step, the first order conditions are reduced to a system of two simultaneous differential equations in Y^* and K^*. The determinant of the characteristic matrix of the system is then evaluated at the steady state; it is found to be negative, and the saddle point property of the equilibrium is thereby established.

Step I: First order conditions

The Hamiltonian of the system is given by:

$$H = e^{-\delta t} \left\{ P \frac{\Phi^*(K^*)}{F(P)} + \Phi \left(\frac{\Phi^*(K^*)}{F(P)} - \lambda^* K^* \right) \right\}$$

and the first order conditions are:

$$\frac{\partial H}{\partial P} = 0 \leftrightarrow Y^* = \frac{F}{F'} - \Phi' - P \qquad (15)$$

$$\frac{\partial H}{\partial K^*} + (e^{-\delta t} Y^*) = 0 \leftrightarrow \dot{Y}^* = (\lambda^* + \delta)Y^* - (P + Y^* + \Phi')\frac{r}{F} \qquad (16)$$

$$\frac{\partial H}{\partial Y} = K^* \leftrightarrow \dot{K}^* = \frac{\Phi^*}{F} - \lambda K^* \qquad (17)$$

$$\lim_{t \to \infty} e^{-\delta t} Y^* = 0 \qquad (18)$$

Equations (16) and (17) govern the rate of change of K^* and Y^* over time, whilst equation (15) governs the terms of trade with K^* and Y^* taken as fixed. Equation (18) is the transversality condition which provides the missing terminal boundary to our differential equation problem.

Consider equation (15). It can be rewritten as:

$$-\Phi' = P\left(1 + \frac{-F}{PF'}\right) + Y^* \qquad (19)$$

where the left hand side has an exact interpretation as the marginal cost of producing a unit of capital goods, whilst the right hand side represents the marginal revenue obtained from selling a unit of capital goods (the expression $\frac{-F}{PF'}$, is simply the reciprocal of the elasticity of the foreign demand curve). Except for dynamic considerations the policy maker acts analogously to a profit maximising monopolist, and this is brought out in figure 1, a familiar diagram.

In this figure, MRs represents the marginal revenue curve of static models, and $MR_S + Y^*$ represent the relevant marginal revenue curve of our policy maker, who accounts for dynamic effects. The pair $(P_C, \bar{Q}_C)$ represents the terms of trade and level of exports associated with a perfectly competitive situation. The pair $(P_S, \bar{Q}_S)$ represents the optimal policy were the DC merely interested in maximising its current income, equating (current) marginal revenue and marginal cost. The pair $(P_D, \bar{Q}_D)$, on the other hand, represents the optimal policy when the DC wishes to maximise an infinite sum of discounted consumption, equating ("total") marginal revenue and marginal cost.

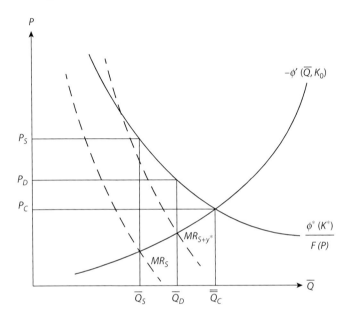

Figure 1 indicates that if $Y^* > 0$, then the optimal trade restriction is always smaller than in static models—i.e. P, the world price of capital goods is lower and $\bar{Q}$, the quantity of capital goods produced and exported is higher.

In fact, it is easy to show that in our model $Y^* > 0$ always along the optimal path. To see this, suppose that at some point along the optimal path $Y^* < 0$. Then since from equation (15)

$$P + Y^* + \Phi'' = \frac{F}{F'} > 0, \text{ equations (16) implies}$$

$$\dot{Y}^* = (\lambda^* + \delta)Y^* - \frac{r}{F'} < \delta Y^* < 0$$

It follows that

$$\frac{\dot{Y}^*}{Y^*} > \delta$$

and that

$$\lim_{t \to \infty} e^{-\delta t} Y^* = -\infty$$

violating the transversality condition for optimality.

From figure (1) we are also led to the conclusions that, other things equal, the higher the shadow price of foreign capital accumulation Y^*, the lower is the optimal terms of trade; also the higher the foreign capital stock K^*, the higher the equilibrium terms of trade.

In fact, total differentiation of condition (19) yields:

$$dY^* = \left\{ \left(\frac{-F''F}{(F')^2} \right) +'' \left(\frac{\Phi^* F'}{F^2} \right) \right\} dP + \left(-\Phi'' \frac{r}{F} \right) dK^* \qquad (20)$$

$$\underbrace{}_{\text{sgn }(-)} \qquad \underbrace{}_{\text{sgn }(+)}$$

This relation will also be of use in step II below.

Step II: Stability of the steady state

Substituting equation (15) into equation (16) we obtain:

$$\dot{Y}^* = (\lambda^* + \delta)Y^* - \frac{r}{F'} \qquad (21)$$

This expression, together with equation (17) forms a system of two first-order differential equations in the unknowns K^* and Y^*: the unknown P also enters the equations, however, and relation (20) is needed in order to study the behaviour of the system at a given point.

We shall now demonstrate that, provided the initial foreign capital stock is in the neighbourhood of the steady state, then the optimal path is unique and converges to the steady state.

This amounts to proving that the steady state is stable in a saddle point sense, and that the unique stable branch of the saddle point (the separatrix) is the only path satisfying all the necessary conditions.

Saddle-point stability is equivalent to the condition that Δ, the determinant of the system, be negative at the point in question[6]:

$$\Delta \equiv \begin{vmatrix} \dfrac{\partial \dot{K}^*}{\partial K} & \dfrac{\partial \dot{K}^*}{\partial Y^*} \\ \\ \dfrac{\partial \dot{Y}}{\partial K^*} & \dfrac{\partial \dot{Y}^*}{\partial Y^*} \end{vmatrix}$$

The sign of the elements of Δ, evaluated at are investigated in the paragraphs (a) to (d) below.

(a) $\quad \dfrac{\partial \dot{Y}^*}{\partial K^*} = -\left(\dfrac{r'F' - f''r \dfrac{\partial P}{\partial K^*}}{(F')^2} \right)$

$\text{sgn} \dfrac{\partial Y^*}{\partial K^*} = \left(-\dfrac{(-) \times (+) - (+) \times (+)}{(+)} \right) = (+)$

(b) $\quad \dfrac{\partial \dot{Y}^*}{\partial Y^*} = \delta + \left\{ \lambda^* - \dfrac{r}{F} \left[1 + (-\Phi'') \left(\dfrac{\Phi}{F''} \right) \left(\dfrac{F'}{F} \right)^3 \right]^{-1} \right\}$

Note that the square bracketed term on the right side is larger than unity. Also note that in the steady state $\lambda = \dfrac{\Phi^*/K^*}{F} > \dfrac{r}{F}$ by virtue of the concavity of the foreign production function. It follows that $\text{sgn} \dfrac{\partial \dot{Y}^*}{\partial Y^*} = (+)$

(c) $\quad \dfrac{\partial \dot{K}^*}{\partial Y^*} = \dfrac{-\Phi^* F'}{F^2} \dfrac{\partial P}{\partial Y^*}$

$\text{sgn} \dfrac{\partial K^*}{\partial Y^*} = -\dfrac{(+) \times (+)}{(+)} \times (-) = (+)$

---

[6] This implies that the characteristic roots are both real, and opposite in sign.

$$\text{(d)} \quad \frac{\partial \dot{K}^*}{\partial K^*} = \frac{r}{F} - \lambda^* - \frac{F^1 \Phi^* \dfrac{\partial P}{\partial K^*}}{F^2}$$

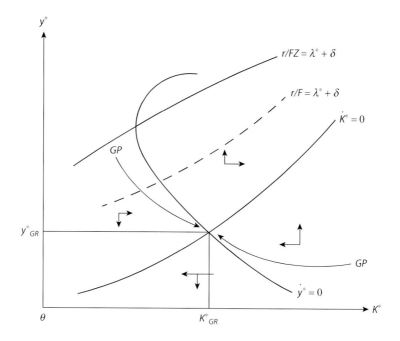

Note that, in the steady state, $\lambda \dfrac{\Phi^*/K^*}{F} > \dfrac{r}{F}$. Also note that the third term in the above expression is positive since $\dfrac{\partial P}{\partial K^*} > 0$. It follows that,

$$\text{sgn} \frac{\partial \dot{K}^*}{\partial K^*} = (-)$$

The sign of Δ is thus given by:

$$\text{sgn } \Delta = ((-) \times (+)) - ((+) \times (+)) = (-)$$

completing the proof that the steady state is stable in a saddle point sense.

The phase diagram, indicating the movement of Y^* and K^* along the optimal path is given in figure II. The stable branch of the saddle point, the Golden Path (GP in figure II), is characterised by a monotonic fall in Y^* and a monotonic rise in K^* when $K_0^* < K_{GR}^*$, the "golden rule" steady state level of the foreign capital stock.

d. The evolution of the export tax and the transfer criterion along the optimal path.

If the initial LDC capital stock is close to but below its steady state value, it is easy to demonstrate that there is a steady increase in P, the world price of capital goods, along the optimal path. To see this, note that from equation (20),

$$\frac{dP}{dY^*} < 0, \qquad \frac{dP}{K^*} > 0$$

but along the optimal path $\dot{Y}^* < 0$ and $\dot{K}^* > 0$; it follows immediately that $\dot{P} > 0$. This result permits us to characterise the path of the export tax and the transfer criterion along the optimal path.

(i) The export tax

In this model it turns out to be more convenient computationally to consider a tax on the export of capital goods (T), defined as a percentage of the world price of capital goods, rather than a tariff on the imports of consumption goods. The reader can easily verify that there exists a one-to-one monotonic relation between the two policy instruments ($\theta = T/(1-T)$)

To derive the optimal export tax (T), note that the return facing competitive producers of capital goods at home is P, but the true social return is $P + Y^* - F/F'$ (see condition (15)). It follows that the required export tax (T) is given by:

$$P(1-T) = P + Y^* - \frac{F}{F'}$$

which implies:

$$T = \frac{1}{\varepsilon} - \frac{Y^*}{P} \qquad (22)$$

where ε is PF'/F the elasticity of the foreign demand curve. The term $1/\varepsilon$ is a "static" component, and the term Y^*/P is a dynamic component.

We have immediately the following result; along the optimal path (assuming $K_0^{\cdot} < K_{GR}^{\cdot}$), the dynamic component (a subsidy) of the export tax decreases monotonically, since Y^* falls and P rises monotonically. If the elasticity ε is constant (as in the C.E.S. case) or falling in P, the optimal trade policy is to set a low export tax at first (perhaps a subsidy) to let the foreign country grow, and to increase the export tax as the steady state is reached.

(ii) The transfer criterion

The transfer criterion introduced in previous sections:

$$t = \frac{Y - Y^*}{Y} = 1 - \frac{Y^*}{Y}$$

indicates the "true cost" of a transfer. It cannot be directly applied in our model since we do not have a shadow price Y for home capital accumulation. The cost of a unit of home capital in our model is clearly $-\Phi'$, which is the opportunity cost in terms of consumption goods.[7] The relevant transfer criterion becomes:

$$t = 1 - \frac{Y^*}{-\Phi'} \tag{23}$$

Using condition (15), our criterion may be rewritten:

$$t = 1 - \frac{-\Phi' - \dfrac{F}{F'} - P}{-\Phi'} = \frac{P}{-\Phi'}\left(1 - \frac{1}{\varepsilon}\right)$$

since $\varepsilon > 1$ is a second order requirement, we obtain:

$$1 > t > 0$$

so that in this model transfers are always overeffected, but never "at gain," i.e. the DC never actually gains by giving the LDC country a gift.

---

7   This can be obtained directly from equation (6a), setting $U_C = 1$ and $F_{\bar{Q}} = \Phi'$.

We shall now demonstrate that, along the optimal path, the true cost of a transfer t increases, provided the elasticity of the foreign offer curve is constant. By definition,

$$P(1 - T) = -\Phi'$$

and t may be written

$$t = \frac{1}{1-T}\left(1 - \frac{1}{\varepsilon}\right)$$

It was demonstrated in the previous section that, if ε is constant, the optimal export tax T increases monotonically along the optimal path—it follows immediately that t also increases monotonically.

The first step in this comparative statics analysis is the evaluation of the sign of the determinant of the 3 × 3 matrix on the left hand side, denoted

$$\Delta = \frac{rF''}{F'}\left(\frac{r}{F} - \lambda^*\right) + \frac{\Phi^*}{F^2}(-r_{K^*}) + A(\lambda^* + \delta)\left(\lambda^* - \frac{r}{F}\right) + \left(-\Phi''\frac{r}{F}\right)(\lambda^* + \delta)\left(\frac{\Phi^* F'}{F^2}\right)$$

All the terms which comprise Δ are positive with the exception of the term $-\frac{rF''}{F'}\lambda^*$. We have, however, $A > \frac{F''F}{(F')^2}$ (by definition of A) and, also

$$\frac{F''F}{(F')^2}(\lambda^* + \delta)\left(\lambda^* - \frac{r}{F}\right) > -\frac{rF''}{F'}\lambda^* > 0$$

To see this, note that the above expression can be rewritten:

$$\frac{\lambda^* F''F}{(F')^2}\left(\lambda^* + \delta - \frac{r}{F}\right) > 0,$$

a positive expression since in the steady state $\lambda^* > \frac{r}{F}$, in view of the concavity of the foreign production function.

We thus have $\Delta > 0$.

40 TRADE PREFERENCES, FOREIGN AID, AND SELF-INTEREST

Now, by Cramer's rule,

$$\Delta \times \frac{dY^*}{d\delta} = \text{Det} \begin{pmatrix} 0 & A & \Phi'' \frac{r}{F} \\ -Y^* & \frac{rF''}{(F')^2} & \frac{-r_{K^*}}{F'} \\ 0 & \frac{-\Phi^* F'}{F^2} & \frac{r}{F} - \lambda^* \end{pmatrix} = AY^* \left(\frac{r}{F} - \lambda^* \right) + \Phi'' \frac{r}{F} \left(\frac{Y'' \Phi^* F'}{F^2} \right)$$

We have $\text{sgn} \dfrac{dY^*}{d\delta} > 0$

Similarly,

$$\Delta \times \frac{dP}{d\delta} = -Y^* (r/F - \lambda^*) > 0$$

and,

$$\Delta \times \frac{dK^*}{d\delta} = Y^* \left(\frac{-\Phi F'}{F^2} \right) < 0$$

Directly from the above inequalities and from the definitions of T (equation 22) and t (equation 23), we have the following result: a rise in the rate of time preference of the DC will, in the steady state, induce

(i) a fall in the LDC's capital stock
(ii) a rise in the export tax on capital goods provided the LDC's offer curve of consumption goods has elasticity constant or falling in price.
(iii) an indeterminate change in the transfer criteria due to a fall in Y^* which may or may not be offset by the fall in $(-\Phi^*)$, the marginal cost of producing capital goods.

2.7. SUMMARY AND CONCLUSIONS

In a trade policy model in which the policy maker of a large country accounts for the effect of his policy on the foreign country's growth, hence his future welfare, we have demonstrated that the optimal tariff prescription has to be amended to at least partially "subsidise" the foreign country if its growth is trade biased. If its growth is anti-trade biased, a transfer of capital is always at least partially recouped.

These conclusions were reached under very general assumptions, as these models go. Under more restrictive assumptions, a special case was analysed in which the foreign country is an LDC whose growth is trade biased, and the home country is a DC constrained to a stationary state. It was found that it is in the interest of the DC to steer the LDC towards a steady state. Along a path beginning below the steady state, the terms of trade, the optimal tariff, and the cost of foreign aid were found to increase monotonically. The latter two results were found to be conditional upon a foreign demand curve with elasticity constant. Under this assumption, it was also found that an increase in the rate of time preference of the DC always induces an increase in the optimal steady state tariff, and an indeterminate change in the cost of foreign aid. The rise in the DC's time preference always induces a fall in the LDC's steady state capital stock.

REFERENCES

Bardhan, P. K., "On Factor Accumulation and the Pattern of International Stabilisation", *Review of Economic Studies,* January 1966.

Johnson, H. G., "The Transfer Problem and Exchange Stability", *Journal of Political Economy,* June 1956.

Kurz, M., "The General Instability of a Class of Competitive Growth Processes", *Review of Economic Studies,* 35, 1968.

Ryder, A., "Optimal Accumulation and Trade in an Open Economy of Moderate Size", in *Essays on the Theory of Optimal Economic Growth,* K. Shell, ed., Cambridge, Massachusetts, MIT Press, 1967.

Samuelson, P. A., "A Catenary Turnpike Theorem Involving Consumption and the Golden Rule", *American Economic Review,* C5, 1965.

CHAPTER 3

A Dynamic Theory of the Optimal Foreign Investment Restriction

3.1. INTRODUCTION

The previous chapter has demonstrated that in a dynamic model in which the home country's trade opportunities are temporally interdependent it is in the interest of a large country to subsidise the foreign country's growth, by effecting outright gifts or lowering the tariffs below the statically optimum level, provided the foreign country's growth is trade biased.

This chapter applies an analytical framework similar to that developed in chapter 2 within the context of a different model. Specifically, we shall deal with a model of international investment without trade and tackle the debated problem of the optimal foreign investment restriction.

Unlike the theory of the optimal tariff, work on the optimal foreign investment tax is of recent vintage. In fact, McDougall (1960) and Jasay (1960) were the first to notice that a large lending country could profit from levying a tax designed to restrict its competitively determined foreign investment, raising its return more than proportionally up to a point. They found (see Section 3.2) that the optimal tax equals the elasticity of the rate of return with respect to foreign investment.

To my knowledge, only two attempts have been made to analyse this issue in a dynamic multiperiod setting. The first attempt, by Negishi, led to the conclusion that if a) an investing country's objective is to maximise steady state income, and b) if only capitalists save, the static model prescription is no longer valid. Negishi's framework, though useful in that it draws attention to dynamic considerations, is unsatisfactory since the two premises upon which his result is based appear rather arbitrary, especially in the light of the theory of optimal economic growth initiated by Ramsey and popularised in the 1960's.

In this respect, the second attempt, by Bardhan, is more satisfactory. Bardhan studied the problem of a large borrowing country facing a static but less than infinitely elastic supply of funds in a Ramsey type framework. His work has drawn little attention largely, I suspect, because his principal result was a confirmation of the static theory: the optimal tax on foreign borrowing equals the elasticity of the foreign lending function. Indeed, Bardhan concluded that this condition is "atemporal".

This chapter demonstrates that the optimal tax prescription first derived from static models, and later confirmed in Bardhan's dynamic framework, is in fact no longer valid when the analysis is carried to a higher level of generality, relaxing the assumption, implicit in Bardhan's framework, that foreign investment opportunities are temporally independent. More specifically, the investing country's policy maker is assumed to account for the effect of his policy on the rate of growth of the other country, hence on his lending terms in the future. It is found that, under plausible assumptions, it is in the enlightened self interest of the policy maker to expand investment beyond the static prescription, so as to reap future gains.

An important advantage of the model of international investment compared to the model of international trade is that it has a fairly simple structure. This allows us to analyse with relative ease: a) the characteristics of the optimal path given different assumptions as to initial and terminal conditions, and planning horizon; b) the relative magnitude of dynamic versus static effects under neoclassical assumptions (Appendix I); c) the implications of a simple assumption about retaliation (Chapter 4).

The remainder of the chapter can be divided into two main parts. The first part, consisting of sections 3.2 and 3.3, contains the derivation of the optimal dynamic tax formula within a general model of international investment. The second part, consisting of section 3.4, analyses in detail a special case in which the home country is a very large developed country and the foreign country is less developed.

3.2. DERIVATION OF THE "STATIC" OPTIMAL TAX

In this section we briefly review the derivation of the optimal foreign investment tax.

The problem of the investing ("home") country is:

$$\text{Max } r(K_F)K_F + F(\bar{K} - K_F)$$
$$K_F$$

Where r is the return per unit of capital invested abroad, K_F, $F(\cdot)$ is the home country's production function and $\bar{K}$ is home country capital, assumed fixed.

The first order condition is given by

$$r + r'K_F = a \leftrightarrow r(1 - r/K_F) = F'$$

where $\eta r/K_F$ is the elasticity of r with respect to K_F defined positive.

Competition (or "arbitrage") implies

$$r = F'$$

We therefore require a tax θ such that

$$r(1 - \theta) = r(1 - \eta r/K_F)$$

Thus

$$\theta = \eta r/K_F$$

This tax formula remains unaltered if we assume that the home country grows, but that the foreign country is static or grows exogenously (Bardhan, 1967).

3.3. DERIVATION OF THE OPTIMAL DYNAMIC FOREIGN INVESTMENT TAX

a. The Model

The home and foreign (* will denote foreign variables, as before) countries produce the same consumption good with different technologies. This same consumption good can be molded costlessly into capital or may be

CHAPTER 3: OPTIMAL FOREIGN INVESTMENT RESTRICTION

consumed. Because of differences in know-how, the capital good of the home and foreign country *can* be different. No trade is allowed. Moreover, it is assumed that only the home country invests abroad, and also there is no labour growth. Both of the latter assumptions are strictly simplifying and could fairly easily be relaxed.

In this chapter, as in chapter 2, it is assumed that the foreign country does not retaliate. This is obviously an assumption which deserves further scrutiny; appendix 2 contains some results about the optimal retaliation policy for a small country which are derived in the context of a static model.

The home country's problem can be set out as follows:

$$\text{Max} \int_0^T e^{-\delta t} u(c) \, dt$$

s.t.
$$c = F((1-\alpha)K) + r(K^*, \alpha K)\alpha K - (\dot{K} + \lambda K)$$
$$\dot{K} = s(F(\cdot) + r(\cdot)\alpha K) - \lambda K$$
$$\dot{K}^* = S^*(K^*, \alpha K) - \lambda^* K^*$$

$$K(0) = K_0 \qquad K^*(0) = K^*_0$$
$$K(T) = K_t \qquad K^*(T) = K^*_t$$
$$0 < \alpha < 1 \qquad 0 < s < 1$$

Notation in order of appearance

$\int(\ )$	=	Welfare Functional
$e^{-\delta t}$	=	Discount Factor
$u(c)$	=	Utility of Consumption
$F(\cdot)$	=	Production Function (home)
α	=	Proportion of Home Capital Invested Abroad
K	=	Total Capital Stock Owned by Home Country
K^*	=	Total Capital Stock Owned by Foreign Country
$\dot{K}$	=	dK/dt
s	=	Proportion of Home Income Saved
$r(\cdot)$	=	Return per Unit of Foreign Investment
S^*	=	Foreign Country's Gross Savings Function

λ^*, λ	=	Depreciation Rates of Foreign and Home Country Respectively
$K(0)$, $K^*(0)$	=	Initial Conditions of Home and Foreign Capital Stock Respectively
$K(T)$, $K^*(T)$	=	Terminal conditions of Home and Foreign Captial Stock Respectively

Using the maximum principle of Pontryagin et al., the necessary conditions* are derived as follows:

Step I Define the Hamiltonian, H:

$$e^{\delta t} H = u(F(\cdot) + r(\cdot)\alpha K)(1-s) + y(s(F(\cdot) + r(\cdot)\alpha K) - \lambda K)$$
$$+ y^*(S^*(K^*, \alpha K) - \lambda^* K^*)$$

Where y and y^* and conjugate variables (functions of time) that have an exact interpretation as shadow prices of K and K^* respectively, i.e.

$$y(0) = \frac{\partial J^*}{\partial K(0)}$$

Where J^1 is the value of the maximised welfare functional.

Step II Characterise the following system of differential equations

$$\frac{\partial H}{\partial s} = 0 \leftrightarrow u'(\cdot) = y \qquad (1)$$

$$\frac{\partial H}{\partial \alpha} = 0 \leftrightarrow u'(\cdot)(-F'(\cdot) + r(1 - \eta r/K_F)) + y^* \eta_{S^*/K_F} S^*/K_F = 0 \qquad (2)$$

$$(e^{-\delta t} y) + \frac{\partial H}{\partial K} = 0 \leftrightarrow (\lambda + \delta)y + u'(\cdot)(-F'(\cdot)) = \dot{y} \qquad (3)$$

(using equations (1) and (2))

---

1 These conditions are usually sufficient under neoclassical assumptions.

CHAPTER 3: OPTIMAL FOREIGN INVESTMENT RESTRICTION

$$(e^{-\delta t} \dot{y}^*) + \frac{\partial H}{\partial K^*} = 0 \leftrightarrow (\lambda^* + \delta - \eta_{S \cdot /K^*} \cdot S^*/K^*) y^* + u'(\cdot) \eta r / K^* \frac{r K_F}{K^*} = \dot{y}^* \quad (4)$$

$$\dot{K} = s(F(\cdot) + r(\cdot)\alpha K) - \lambda K \quad (5)$$

$$\dot{K}^* = S^*(\cdot) - \lambda^* K^* \quad (6)$$

where

$$\eta_{S \cdot /K_F} = \frac{\partial S^*}{\partial K_F} \frac{K_F}{S^*}, \quad \eta_{r/K^*} = \frac{\partial r}{\partial K^*} \frac{K^*}{r}, \quad \eta_{S \cdot /K^*} = \frac{\partial S^*}{\partial K^*} \frac{K^*}{S^*}$$

The system consists of four differential equations, (3)-(6) in the y's and K's plus two conditions (1) and (2) which can be used to eliminate the control variables α and s. We have four boundary conditions, and the problem can in principle be solved to obtain the optimal time path of the control, state and costate variables.

b. The optimal dynamic tax

This is found by observing that competition or arbitrage imply:

$$F' = r$$

But the dynamic optimum requires (equation (2)):

$$F' = r(1 - \eta_{r/K_F}) + \frac{y^*}{u'} \eta_{S \cdot /K_F} S^*/K_F$$

In order to correct the distortion, we require a tax such that

$$r(1 - \theta) = r(1 - \eta_{r/K_F}) + \frac{y^*}{u'} \eta_{S \cdot /K_F} S^*/K_F$$

yielding the following formula for the optimal tax

$$\theta = \eta_{r/K_F} - \frac{y^*}{u'} \eta_{S \cdot /K_F} S^*/r K_F \quad (7)$$

It is composed of a "static" component η_{r/K_F} identical to the tax of static models, which maximises current income, and a dynamic component

$$-\eta_{S^*/K_F} S^*/rK_F \frac{y^*}{u'}$$

which accounts for the effects of the investment restriction on the foreign country's growth.

The sign of the dynamic component is seen to depend on the sign of y^*, the shadow price of the foreign capital stock in the home country's optimal program, and on the sign of η_{S^*/K_F}, the effect of international investment on the foreign country's rate of capital accumulation. If these two quantities have the same sign, the dynamic component of the optimal tax is a subsidy; if the two quantities have opposite signs, the dynamic component of the optimal tax is an additional tax.

In the following subsection the formula for the optimal tax is obtained under the assumption of steady state. This assumption permits us to eliminate the expression y^*/u' from the general expression for the optimal tax (7), and to focus on the underlying structural parameters of the system.

c. The optimal dynamic tax in the steady state

The steady state is defined as the value of the variables α, s, K^*, K, y^*, y which satisfies:

$$\dot{K}^* = \dot{K} = \dot{y}^* = \dot{y} = 0$$

Using these conditions in (3) one obtains:

$$F'(1-\alpha)K - \lambda = \delta \qquad (3')$$

The return on home installed capital satisfies a modified golden rule (Phelps,). Similarly, using (2), (4) and (6), one can show that in the steady state, the "indirect return" from foreign capital accumulation also satisfies a modified golden rule:

$$\eta_{S^*/K_F} + \frac{\eta_{r/K^*} \cdot \eta_{S^*/K_F} \cdot \lambda}{F'(\cdot) - r(1 - \eta_{r/K_F})} - \lambda = \delta \qquad (4')$$

The steady state tax θ_S is given by substituting for y^* in (7), using (4') and (4) above:

$$\theta_S = \eta_{r/K_F} - \frac{\eta_{r/K^*} \cdot \eta_{S\cdot/K_F} \cdot \lambda}{\delta + \lambda(1 - \eta_{S\cdot/K^*})}$$

Usually, in neoclassical growth models $\eta_{S\cdot/K^*} < 1$ (This is a requirement for stability in most models), and therefore

$$\delta + \lambda(1 - \eta_{S\cdot/K^*}) > 0.$$

Given this assumption, we have amongst others, four empirically interesting possibilities:

	K^* and K_F are complementary factors ($\eta_{r/K^*} > 0$)	K^* and K_F are substitute factors ($\eta_{r/K^*} < 0$)
Capitalists and workers abroad save in the same proportion	Dynamic component: A subsidy	Dynamic component: An additional tax
Mostly capitalists save	Dynamic component: A subsidy	Dynamic component: A subsidy

Only in case (2) would we expect the dynamic component to be an additional tax rather than a subsidy.[2]

3.4. ANALYTICAL SOLUTION OF A SPECIAL CASE OF COMPLEMENTARITY

a. Premise

In the trade model of chapter 2 a special case was analysed in detail in which the home country is developed (DC) and the foreign country is less

---

[2] McDougall has shown that when K^* and K_F are competitive a rise in K_F always increases national income if the foreign country's production function is neoclassical and well behaved.

developed (LDC). It was assumed that the LDC's growth is trade biased. In this section we shall analyse another case in which the LDC and DC have a "Common interest" in each other's growth. Specifically, we shall consider a special case of the general foreign investment model, in which the LDC's capital stock is assumed to be complementary to the foreign-invested capital of the DC. Also, the DC is assumed to be "very large". We shall analyse the stability properties of the model and trace the development of the foreign investment tax along the optimal path.

The special case is modelled under two greatly simplifying assumptions:

- The home country is constrained to be in a steady state; we no longer have to consider the control s, state K, and "price" y.
- The foreign country's technology is Cobb-Douglas and its savings are proportional to income.

b. The Model

As in Chapter 2 the LDC's variables will be denoted by stars wherever confusion with DC variables may arise. The LDC production function is given by:

$$\alpha, \ M, \ \beta \ > \ 0$$

$$X^* = AL^{*M} K^{*\alpha} K_F^{\beta}$$

$$\alpha + M + \beta = 1$$

Redefining units so that AL^M (labour is fixed) equals unity, we write

$$X^* = K^{*\alpha} K_F^{\beta}$$

The total return from foreign investment is simply the share of K_F in X^*

$$r(\cdot) K_F = \beta X^*$$

CHAPTER 3: OPTIMAL FOREIGN INVESTMENT RESTRICTION

The static optimal tax is given by

$$\eta_{r/K_F} = \frac{d\frac{\beta X^*}{K_F}}{dK_F} \times \frac{K_F}{\frac{\beta X^*}{K_F}} = 1 - \beta$$

The foreign savings function is

$$S^*(K^*, K_F) = s(M + \alpha)X^*$$

a fixed proportion s of the share of income earned by local factors. The DC's technology (labour fixed) is simply:

$$X = a(K - K_F)$$

where "a" is the constant rate of return to capital in the DC, indicating that the DC is "very large". Both the LDC capital depreciate at rate λ so that[3]

$$\dot{K}^* = s(\alpha + M(X^* - \lambda K^*)$$

and

$$\dot{K} = S - \lambda K$$

We shall assume that S, the DC's gross savings, are constrained equal to depreciation

$$S = \lambda K_0$$

Where K_0 is the DC initial capital stock. The DC is thus constrained to a stationary state. The computer simulations of a more general model in which the DC can grow but is "close" to a steady state showed no significant deviation from the behaviour of this simple model (see Appendix 1). The home country utility is simply:

$$u(c) = c$$

---

3 This assumption is easily relaxed.

The home country consumption is given by:

$$c = a(K_0 - K_F) + \beta X^* - \lambda K_0$$

c. The relation between tax, foreign investment and foreign capital stock

Given a tax on foreign investment θ, arbitrage will induce equality between the DC and LDC rates of return

$$(1 - \theta)\frac{\beta X^*}{K_F} - \lambda = a - \lambda$$

This yields the following simple relation

$$K_F = \left(\frac{1}{a}\beta(1-\theta)K^{*\alpha}\right)^{1/1-\beta} \tag{1}$$

As is intuitively plausible foreign investment increases in K^* and decreases in "a" and θ.

In (θ, K^*) space iso-K_F curves may be drawn (Fig. 1)

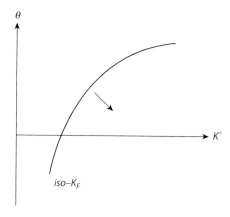

with the arrow indicating increasing quantities of K_F. This relation will be of use in later sections.

d. Formulation of the problem

The DC's problem can be set out as follows:

$$\text{Max} \int_0^T e^{-\delta t} (a(K_0 - K_F) + \beta X^* - \lambda K_0) \, dt$$

Subject to

RELATION	DESCRIPTION
$x^* = K^{*\alpha} K_F^\beta$	Definitional relations
$K_F = \left(\dfrac{1}{\alpha}\beta(1-\theta)K^{*\alpha}\right)^{1/1-\beta}$	
$\dot{K}^* = s(\alpha + M)X^* - \lambda K^*$	
$K^*(0) = K_0'$, $\quad K^*(T) = K_T'$	Motion of foreign capital stock
	Initial and terminal conditions
$\underline{\theta} \leq \theta \leq 1$	Condition on θ

This problem is a special case of the general formulation given in the previous section. However, instead of directly controlling the share of home owned capital, which is invested abroad, here the government is allowed to control the tax rate θ. This, we believe, will make it easier to relate intuitively to the results of the model.

The lower bound $\underline{\theta} < 0$ represents the "politically feasible" maximum subsidy to foreign investment[4].

In our solution we shall *assume* that K_0 and $\underline{\theta}$ are such that $K_F < K_0$ always. This amounts to an assumption that K_0 is large enough.

e. Solution of the problem

Our objective is an approximate characterisation of the path of the tax rate θ, and the foreign capital stock K^* under different assumptions on boundary conditions.

---

4 Setting a bound θ, absolves us from the more "natural" $\theta > \theta^*$ where θ^* solves $K_F(\theta^*, K^*) = K_0$; such formulation would take us beyond the problems studied by Pontryagin et al. since the domain of control depends on the state variable.

Define the Hamiltonian

$$H(K^*, y^*, \theta) = e^{-\delta t}\{a(K_0 - K_F) + \beta X^* - \lambda K_0 \\ + y^*(s(\alpha + M)X^* - \lambda K^*)\}$$

The conditions for an optimum are given by

$$\underline{\theta} \leq \theta \leq 1 \quad \text{when} \quad \frac{\partial H}{\partial \theta} = 0 \tag{2a}$$

$$\theta = 1 \quad \text{when} \quad \frac{\partial H}{\partial \theta} < 0 \tag{2b}$$

$$\theta = 0 \quad \text{when} \quad \frac{\partial H}{\partial \theta} < 0 \tag{2c}$$

Also

$$(e^{-\delta t}) + \frac{\partial H}{\partial K^*} = 0 \tag{3}$$

and

$$\dot{K}^* = S^*(\cdot) - \lambda K^* \tag{4}$$

In order to keep track of the rather laborious calculations, we outline the strategy of the solution:

Step 1

Use equation (4) which is of the form $\dot{K}^* = G(\theta, K^*)$ to characterize $\dot{K}^* = 0$ in the phase space (θ, K^*)

Step 2

Use relations (2) to find the optimal tax as a function of y^* only.

CHAPTER 3: OPTIMAL FOREIGN INVESTMENT RESTRICTION

Step 3

Use the relation obtained from step 2, to substitute θ for y^* in (3) obtaining:

$$\dot{\theta} = H(\theta, K^*)$$

Step 4

Characterize $\dot{\theta} = H(\cdot)$ in the phase space (θ, K^*).

Step 5

Characterise the movement of the system in (θ, K^*) space given

$$\dot{\theta} = H(\cdot)$$

$$\dot{K}^* = G(\cdot), \text{ and boundaries.}$$

Step 1 - Characterization of $\dot{K}^* = 0$

Equation (4), together with the definitional relations yields:

$$\dot{K}^* = s(\alpha + M)\left(\frac{1}{a} - \beta(1-\theta)\right)^{\beta/1-\beta} K^{*\alpha/1-\alpha} - \lambda K^*$$

Setting $\dot{K}^* = 0$ we obtain the steady state level of the LDC's capital stock as a function of the DC's investment tax $(K_S^{\cdot}(\theta))$.

$$K_S^{\cdot}(\theta) = (\lambda^{-1}s(\alpha + M))^{1-\beta/1-(\alpha+\beta)} \cdot \left(\frac{1}{a}\right)^{\beta/1-(\alpha+\beta)} (1-\theta)^{\beta/1-(\alpha+\beta)}$$

As expected, $K_S^{\cdot}(\theta)$ is increasing in s and decreasing in and "a"; it can be verified that

$$\frac{\partial K_S^{\cdot}}{\partial \theta} < 0$$

$$\theta = 1 \leftrightarrow K_S^{\cdot} = 0$$

$$\theta = \underline{\theta} \leftrightarrow K_S^{\cdot} > 0$$

We can draw (Fig. 2), $K_S^\cdot(\theta)$

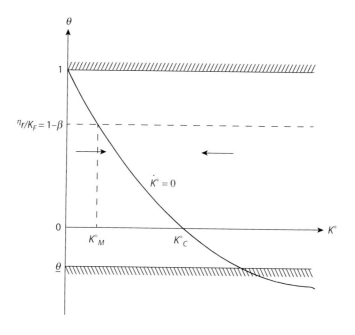

The motion of the system off the $\dot{K}^* = 0$ locus may be determined by noting that a Taylor expansion around $K_S^\cdot$ yields

$$\dot{K}^*(K^*) = \frac{\partial \dot{K}^*}{\partial K^*}(K_S^\cdot)(K^* - K_S^\cdot)$$

$$\left(\frac{\alpha}{1-\beta} S^*(K_S^\cdot) - \lambda K_S^\cdot\right) \frac{1}{K_S^\cdot}(K^* - K_S^\cdot)$$

Note that in the steady state, $S^* = \lambda K^*$ and that $\frac{\alpha}{1-\beta} < 1$, it follows that

$$\dot{K}^* < 0 \leftrightarrow K^* > K_S^\cdot$$

Moreover, for given θ, it is easy to verify that the equilibrium $K_S^\cdot(\theta)$ is globally stable and unique since the system is analogous to the Solow-Swan framework and satisfies the well-known Inada conditions. The arrows in

CHAPTER 3: OPTIMAL FOREIGN INVESTMENT RESTRICTION

Figure 2 are drawn to indicate that, from any point in the phase space, if θ is given, the system converges to $\dot{K}_S(\theta)$.

The point $\dot{K}_M$ indicates the level of steady state capital in the foreign country given that the home country adopts perenially a tax policy to maximise its current level of consumption. The point $\dot{K}_C$ corresponds to the long run competitive equilibrium, when $\theta = 0$.

Step 2 - Expressing θ_0 (θ Optimal) as a function of y^*

We have

$$\frac{\partial H}{\partial \theta} = \frac{\partial H}{\partial K_F} \times \frac{\partial K_F}{\partial \theta}$$

$$= \left(\frac{\beta X^*}{K_F} (\beta + y^* s(\alpha + M)) - a \right) \times \frac{\partial K_F}{\partial \theta}$$

Case 1 $\underline{\theta} < \theta_0 < 1$

In this case, $\dfrac{\partial K_F}{\partial \theta} < 0$ always (see eq. 1) and consequently

$$\frac{\partial H}{\partial \theta} = 0 \leftrightarrow \frac{\beta X^*}{K_F}(\beta + y^* s(\alpha + M)) = 0$$

Using (1) to substitute for K_F in (5), one obtains

$$\theta_0 = (1 - \beta) - s(\alpha + M)y^*, \tag{6}$$

which precisely corresponds to the formula for the dynamic tax obtained in the general formulation:

$$\theta_0 = \eta_{r/K_F} - \frac{y^*}{u'} \eta_{S \cdot / K_F} \frac{S^*}{r(\cdot)K_F}$$

as is easy to verify (Take $u'(\cdot) = 1$).

The relation (6) is represented in Figure 3:

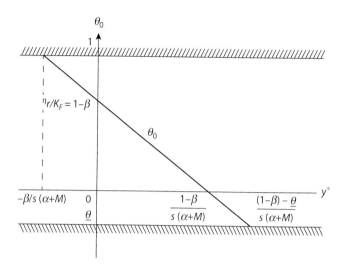

Note that the optimal static tax is adopted, $\theta_0 = 1 - \beta$ only when the shadow price of foreign capital accumulation is 0.

On the other hand, a laissez-faire ($\theta_0 = 0$) policy is adopted whey $y^* = \dfrac{1-\beta}{s(\alpha + M)}$; this is the only case where the unperceived opportunity for "static" monopoly gains is exactly offset by the unperceived opportunity of "dynamic" gains.

Case 2: $\theta = 1$
From Figure 3, this case occurs when $y^* < \dfrac{-\beta}{s(\alpha + M)}$; in fact, in this case $\dfrac{\partial H}{\partial K_F} < 0$ always as is easily verified by substituting for y^* in $\dfrac{\partial H}{\partial K_F}$.

This is a case where the dynamic loss from investing abroad is so high as to offset any possible static gains. Why should the home country ever incur a "dynamic" loss from investing abroad? This question will be addressed in subsection h(iii) below.

CHAPTER 3: OPTIMAL FOREIGN INVESTMENT RESTRICTION

Case 3: $\theta = \underline{\theta}$
This occurs when

$$y^* > \frac{(1-\beta) - \underline{\theta}}{s(\alpha + M)}$$

in this case

$$\frac{\partial H}{\partial K_F} > a$$

always, the maximum subsidy must be used to induce investors to reap the unperceived dynamic gain.

Step 3 Obtaining $\dot{\theta}_0 = H(\theta_0, K^*)$
Using the expression for θ_0 ((6) above), we derive both sides with respect to time and obtain

$$\dot{\theta}_0 = -s(\alpha + M)\dot{y}^* \qquad \underline{\theta} < \theta < 1$$

From condition (3) we derive the rate of change of y^* along the optimal path

$$\dot{y}^* - \delta y^* + \left(\beta + y^* s(\alpha + M) \frac{\alpha X^*}{K^*} - \lambda y^* \right) = 0 \qquad (6')$$

Substituting θ_0 for y^* one obtains

$$\dot{\theta} = (\lambda + \delta)(\theta - (1-\beta)) + s(\alpha + M)(1-\theta)\alpha \left(\frac{1}{a}(1-\theta) \right)^{\beta/1-\beta_K \cdot -\gamma} \qquad (7)$$

where

$$\gamma = \frac{1 - (\alpha + \beta)}{1 - \beta}$$

Note that $0 < \gamma < 1$.

Step 4 Characterizing $\dot{\theta}_0 = H(\theta_0, K^*)$ in (θ_0, K^*) space

Setting $\dot{\theta} = 0$ in (7), one obtains a relation between the LDC's capital stock and the DC's optimal steady state tax:

$$(1 - \theta)(\lambda + \delta) - \beta(\lambda + \delta) = \frac{\beta^* s(\alpha + M)\alpha \left(\frac{1}{a}\right)^{\beta/1-\beta} (1 - \theta)^{1/1-\beta}}{K^*} \qquad (8)$$

define the following convenient transformation

$$F(K^*) = \frac{1}{K^{*\gamma}}$$

where
$\quad F'(\cdot) < 0 \quad$ for $K^* > 0$
$\quad F > 0 \quad$ for $K^* > 0$

also define

$$Z = s(\alpha + M)\left(\frac{1}{a} - \beta\right)^{\beta/1-\beta} > 0.$$

Using these definitions (8) can be written

$$F = \frac{\lambda + \delta}{Z}\left(\frac{1}{(1-\theta)^{\beta/1-\beta}} - \frac{\beta}{(1-\theta)^{1/1-\beta}}\right) \qquad (8')$$

Deriving with respect to θ we have

$$\frac{dK^*}{d\theta} = \frac{dK^*}{dF}\frac{dF}{d\theta} = -\frac{1}{\gamma}F^{\frac{-1}{\gamma}-1}\left(\frac{\lambda + \delta}{Z}\right)\left(\frac{\frac{\beta}{1-\beta}(1-\theta)^{\frac{2\beta-1}{1-\beta}}}{(1-\theta)^{2-\beta/1-\beta}} - \frac{\frac{\beta}{1-\beta}(1-\theta)^{\frac{\beta}{1-\beta}}}{(1-\theta)^{2/1-\beta}}\right)$$

From the above expressions we obtain directly the following results:

$$\operatorname{sgn}\frac{dK^*}{d\theta} = -\operatorname{sgn}\left(\frac{1}{(1-\theta)^{1/1-\beta}} - \frac{1}{(1-\theta)^{2-\beta/1-\beta}}\right) \qquad (8'')$$

CHAPTER 3: OPTIMAL FOREIGN INVESTMENT RESTRICTION

$$\frac{dK^*}{d\theta} = 0 \leftrightarrow \theta = 0 \tag{9}$$

$$\theta = 0 \leftrightarrow F = \frac{\lambda + \delta}{Z}(1 - \beta) > 0 \qquad K^* > 0 \tag{10}$$

$$\lim_{\theta \to 1-\beta} F = 0 \qquad \lim_{\theta \to 1-\beta} K^* = \infty \tag{11}$$

The latter result is obtained by substituting $\theta = 1 - \xi$ in F in (8'). We also have,

$$\lim_{\theta \to -\infty} F = 0 \qquad \lim_{\theta \to -\infty} K^* = \infty \tag{12}$$

The information contained in (8''), (9), (10), (11) and (12) together with continuity, is sufficient to draw the locus $\dot{\theta} = 0$ in Figure 4.

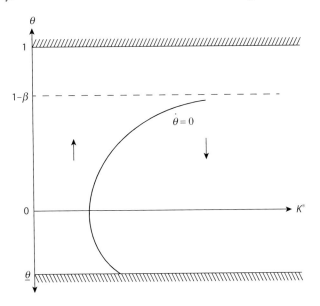

The arrows in Figure 4 indicate the direction of movement of the system. To verify this locally, denote $K^*_{\dot{\theta}=0}$ the value of K^* which ensures $\dot{\theta} = 0$ for given θ and consider the Taylor expansion

$$\dot{\theta}(K^*) = \dot{\theta}\left(K^*_{\dot{\theta}=0}\right) + \frac{\delta\theta}{\delta K^*}\left(K^*_{\dot{\theta}=0}\right)\left(K^* - K^*_{\dot{\theta}=0}\right)$$

$$= -\delta Z(1-\theta)^{1/1-\beta}K^*_{\dot{\theta}=0} - (\gamma + 1)\left(K^* - K^*_{\dot{\theta}=0}\right)$$

since $\gamma > 0$, we have the following relation

$$\dot{\theta}(K^*) > 0 \leftrightarrow K^* < K^*_{\dot{\theta}=0}$$

Step 5 Characterisation of the optimal path
Superimposing Figure 2 and Figure 4 provides the phase diagram of the complete system, Figure 5.

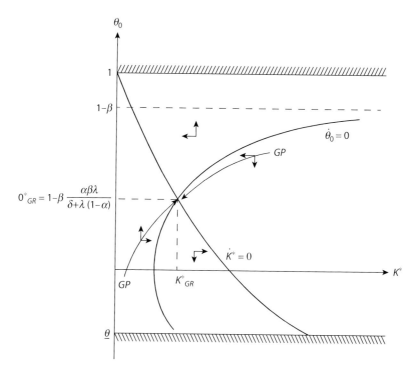

f. The steady state tax

The curves $\dot{\theta}_0 = 0$ and $\dot{K}^* = 0$ have been drawn to cross only once, and with θ^*_{GR}, the long run equilibrium tax rate, positive. That this is in fact justified is most easily seen by applying the formula for the steady state tax developed in the formulation of the general model.

$$\theta^*_{GR} = \eta_{r/K_F} - \frac{\eta_{s^*/K_F^*} \eta_{r/K^*} \cdot \lambda}{\delta + \lambda(1 - \eta_{s/K^*})} = (1 - \beta) - \frac{\beta \alpha \lambda}{\delta + \lambda(1 - \alpha)}$$

CHAPTER 3: OPTIMAL FOREIGN INVESTMENT RESTRICTION

and noting that under the assumptions of our model

$$0 \ll \beta < 1, \quad 0 < \alpha < 1, \quad \alpha + \beta < 1, \quad 1 > \delta > 0, \quad 0 < \lambda < 1$$

we have

$$\theta^{\cdot}_{GR} > 0$$

Thus, *the steady state optimal tax lies between the static tax $(1 - \beta)$ and the laissex-faire policy $\theta_0 = 0$.*

It is also interesting to note that *the optimal tax is closer to the static tax the higher the rate of time preference.*

g. The stability of the Golden Rule Equilibrium: Analytical Verification

Figure 5 suggests that the GR equilibrium (Golden Rule) is a saddle point. The unique stable branch is drawn as GP (Golden Path).

That the equilibrium is locally a saddle point can be verified analytically noting that the determinant of the system Δ is negative

$$\operatorname{sgn} \Delta : \begin{vmatrix} \overset{(-)}{\dfrac{\partial \dot{K}^*}{\partial K^*}} & \overset{(-)}{\dfrac{\partial \dot{K}^*}{\partial \theta^*}} \\ \dfrac{\partial \dot{\theta}}{\partial K^*} & \dfrac{\partial \dot{\theta}}{\partial \theta^*} \\ \underset{(-)}{} & \underset{(+)}{} \end{vmatrix} = ((-) \times (+)) - ((-(X(-) = (-))$$

so that the characteristic roots are real and opposite in sign. The sign of $\dfrac{\partial \dot{K}^*}{\partial K^*}$ and $\dfrac{\partial \dot{\theta}}{\partial K^*}$ were investigated in Steps 1 and 3 respectively. The sign of $\dfrac{\partial \dot{K}^*}{\partial \theta}$ is verified to be negative by direct differentiation of the expression for $\dot{K}^*$ in Step 1. The sign of $\dfrac{\partial \dot{\theta}}{\partial \theta}$ is obtained indirectly by noting that in

Figure 4, $\dfrac{d\theta}{dK^*_{\dot\theta=0}}$ was found > 0 for $\theta > 0$ (analytically, this was obtained from (8''), (9), (11) and the continuity property of the relation). However

$$\frac{d\theta}{dK^*_{\dot\theta=0}} = -\frac{\dfrac{\partial \dot\theta}{\partial K^*}}{\dfrac{\partial \dot\theta}{\partial \theta}}$$

$$\operatorname{sgn}\frac{\partial \dot\theta}{\partial \theta} = (-) \times \operatorname{sgn}\frac{d\theta}{dK^*} \times \operatorname{sgn}\frac{\partial \dot\theta}{\partial K^*}$$

$$= (-) \times (+) \times (-) = (+)$$

h. Analysis of the optimal path under various assumptions

In this section, we shall characterise the optimal path under different assumptions as to the length of the planning horizon, and as to initial and terminal capital stock of the LDC.

Case 1: Infinite time horizon; $K^*(T)$ is free

(i) Optimality of the Golden Path

Here we assume that the planning horizon is infinite and that the terminal K^* is left free. In order to solve the system, we need a terminal condition; this is given by the "transversality condition"

$$\lim_{t \to \infty} e^{-\delta t} y^*(t) = 0$$

Given an initial capital stock in the foreign country $K^*(0)$, one can deduce from Figure 5 that any initial tax $\theta(0)$ which does not lie on the Golden Path (the stable branch of the saddle point) must converge to one of two alternative equilibria:

- if $\theta(0)$ lies above GP the system converges to $\theta = 1$, $K^* = 0$
- if $\theta(0)$ lies below GP the system converges to $\theta = \underline{\theta}$, $K^* = K^*(\underline{\theta})$

CHAPTER 3: OPTIMAL FOREIGN INVESTMENT RESTRICTION

We shall show that neither equilibrium satisfies the transversality condition. In the case $\theta > 1$, $K^* = 0$ equation (6') in Step 3 implies:

$$\frac{\dot{y}^*}{y^*} = \lambda + \delta$$

Also, from Figure 3

$$y^*(h) = \frac{-\beta}{s(\alpha + M)}$$

where h denotes the time when the equilibrium $\theta = 1$, $K^* = 0$ is reached. It follows that

$$y^*(t) = \frac{-\beta}{s(\alpha + M)} e^{(\lambda + \delta)(t - h)}$$

and

$$e^{-\delta t} y^*(t) = \frac{-\beta}{s(\alpha + M)} (e^{\lambda t + (\delta + \lambda)(-h)})$$

and

$$\lim_{t \to \infty} e^{-\delta t} y^*(t) = -\infty$$

In the case $\theta = \underline{\theta}$, $K^* = K^*(\underline{\theta})$ equation (6') implies

$$\frac{\dot{y}^*}{y^*} = \delta + \left(\lambda - s(\alpha + M)\frac{\alpha X^*}{K^*}\right) - \frac{\beta \alpha X^*}{y^* K^*}$$

Since $K^*(\underline{\theta})$ is a steady state, we can write

$$\frac{\dot{y}^*}{y^*} = \delta + \lambda(1 - \alpha) - \frac{\beta \alpha X^*}{y^* K^*}$$

Solving this differential equation, we obtain

$$y^*(t) = C e^{(\delta + \lambda)(1 - \alpha)(t - i)} + \text{Constant}$$

where $C = \dfrac{(1-\beta) - \theta}{s(\alpha + M)}$ from Figure 3 and "i" denotes the time when the $\theta = \underline{\theta}$, $K^* = K^*(\underline{\theta})$ equilibrium is reached. By an argument similar to the above:

$$\lim_{\to \infty} e^{-\delta t} y(t) = \infty$$

The case $\theta = \theta_{GR}$ and $K^* = K^*_{GR}$

In this case the transversality condition is clearly satisfied, since the equilibrium is in the interior region, where $\dot{\theta} = 0$ $y^* =$ Constant.

(ii) The movement of the system along the Golden Path

We shall consider only the case $K^*(0) < K^*_{GR}$. In this case, from Figure 5, one can characterise the time path of both K^* and θ_0 as monotonically increasing. The lower $K^*(0)$, the lower is the initial optimal tax $\theta(0)$, and since (I suspect, but have no rigorous proof) the golden path has an asymptote at $K^* = 0$, the optimal initial tax can be a subsidy. One cannot tell, from Figure 5 whether $K_{F_{GR}} > K_F(0)$, i.e. whether there is a net increase in foreign investment along the Golden Path, since the effect of a rise in K^* (which raises r) is offset by the rise in θ. Along the Golden Path, the dynamic component of the tax (which is a subsidy) decreases steadily as the "marginal productivity" of foreign capital decreases.

The optimal policy for the home country may be summarised as follows: *given a low initial LDC capital stock, set a low tax (perhaps a subsidy) in order to finance the LDC's growth and reap higher returns in the future—as the LDC capital stock increases the private return to foreign investment increases and there will be a tendency to increase foreign investment—however, the higher LDC capital stock also implies less opportunity for dynamic gains, and the tax must be raised to account for this.*

As is well known, the importance of the Golden Path lies not only in the fact that it is the solution to the "pure" case ($T = \infty$, $K^*(\infty)$ free), but also that it exhibits the Turnpike Property (Samuelson, 1965). Roughly speaking, this states that given *any* boundary condition, the optimal path tends to "stay close" to the Golden Path. This property will be exhibited in the remaining problems below.

Case 2 "Altruistic Foreign Policy"

Here we shall consider a case where $K^*(0)$ is "low", but where the DC's government wishes the terminal capital stock of the LDC to be "high" either out of concern for the other country's citizens, or out of concern for future generations. By a "high" capital stock we intend a capital stock which is higher than the competitively determined LDC steady state capital stock (K_C^* in Figure 6). The "type" of optimal path is given below, indicated by P_1 in Figure 6, where $K^*(0)$ and $K^*(T)$ denote possible initial and terminal LDC capital stocks respectively.

The essential property of this path is that the initial tax is low and may even be a subsidy; it rises at first, achieves a maximum and then falls off and *must* become a subsidy. Foreign investment is approximately steady at first but *must* increase monotonically in the final lap.

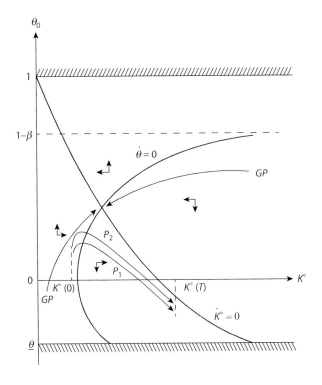

Given a longer time horizon, the home economy can afford to "stay closer" to the Golden Path, where the movement of K^* is slower (Samuelson, 1965). This path is indicated by the in Figure 6.

Thus, the optimal policy is to adopt a tax-path which is as close as possible to the Golden Path, described in the previous section, and then to veer off to meet the terminal constraint.

An interesting extension of the above argument which the reader can easily verify from Figure 5 is:

Given that $\dot{K}_T^* > \dot{K}_0^*$, and given T,

$$\frac{d\theta^{K^*}}{d\dot{K}_T^*} < 0$$

where θ^{K^*} is the tax corresponding to a given K^* on the optimal path.

This simply indicates that the higher the average rate of growth of the LDC desired over the planning horizon, the lower the optimal tax rate corresponding to any level of the foreign capital stock K^*.

Case 3 "Preparation for war"

Here we consider a case where the home country imposes a terminal constraint on its program $K^*(T)$ $(< K^*(0))$ very low, with T very short. A path of this type is depicted in Figure 7. It is in the "top" region of the diagram, where accumulation in the LDC is fastest (LDC savings are lowest).

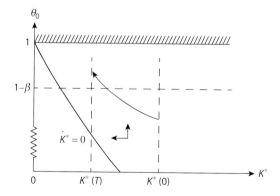

The interesting fact about this path is that it enters the region where $\theta > 1 - \beta$, i.e., where the dynamic component of the optimal tax is negative. This implies that $y^* < 0$, the shadow price of LDC capital accumulation is negative. How can this be? The explanation lies in the fact that in order to meet the terminal constraint, foreign investment is restricted below the point where it maximises current consumption. The higher the initial LDC capital stock in this case, the lower the "value" of the DC's program.

3.5. SUMMARY AND CONCLUSION

We have demonstrated that the static foreign investment tax has to be amended to account for the effects of the policy on future periods. The key factors which affect the relation between the static and the dynamic tax are first, foreign savings behavior, and second, the elasticity of substitution between home and foreign capital in the foreign country's production function. Under the assumption that home and foreign capital are complementary factors the static tax is higher than optimal for plausible foreign savings functions. If, on the other hand, the capital of the home and foreign country are substitute factors, then the static tax is below optimum if foreign capitalists and workers save in the same proportion, but above optimum if mainly capitalists save.

The analytical solution of a special case in which a DC's and an LDC's capital are *complementary* factors revealed that the lower the LDC capital stock in relation to its steady state value, the larger the dynamic offset to the static tax, which may perhaps be a subsidy. The interesting conclusion is that it may not be in the long run interest of a large developed country to restrict its investment in a less developed country in the early stages of its development.

REFERENCES

Bardhan, P. K., "Optimum Foreign Borrowing" in K. Shell (below).
Intriligator, M. D., *Mathematical Optimisation and Economic Theory*, Prentice Hall, 1971.
Jasay, A. E., "The Social Choice Between Home and Overseas Investment", *Economic Journal*, Vol. 98, 1960.
Negishi, T., "Foreign Investment and the Long Run National Advantage", *Economic Record*, December 1965.
McDougall, G. D. A., "The Benefits and Costs of Private Investment from Abroad", *Economic Record*, March 1960.

Phelps, E. S., "The Golden Rule of Accumulation: A Fable for Growthmen", *American Economic Review*, Vol. 51, 1961.
Pontryagin, L. S., et al., *The Mathematical Theory of Optimal Processes*, New York, 1962.
Samuelson, P. A., "A Catenary Turnpike Theorem Involving Consumption and the Golden Rule", *American Economic Review*, 55, 1965.
Shell, K. (ed.), *Essays on the Theory of Optimal Economic Growth*, Cambridge, 1967.

APPENDIX TO CHAPTER 3[1]

SOME SUGGESTIVE RESULTS OBTAINED FROM COMPUTER SIMULATIONS

1. We have devoted much attention to the directions of change induced by the dynamic effects emphasised in this thesis. It now seems appropriate to provide the reader with some inkling as to the order of magnitude of these effects in a neoclassical framework. Specifically, we need answers to the following questions:
   (i) Should the optimal static tax by substantially altered?
   (ii) Does the "social" cost of a transfer differ substantially from its immediate cost?

   From the results of several computer simulations of the foreign investment model we can provide a necessarily incomplete answer:
   In our neoclassical framework, and assuming plausible values of parameters:
   (i) The static component of the optimal tax is nearly always the dominant component, although the dynamic component is often significant.
   (ii) The true cost of a transfer is nearly always very significantly different from its immediate cost, and sometimes (in the complementarity case) the investing country actually *gains* by effecting a transfer.

2. Consider, for example, the simulation of a model of complementarity identical to that analysed in section 3.4 with the following alterations: (a) the DC is allowed to grow, so that savings are adjusted optimally and (b) the DC's production function is of the more general form $x = a(K - K_F)^\gamma$, (c) the DC's utility function is of the more general form $u(c) = \dfrac{c^{1-\tau}}{1-\tau}$.

---

[1] This appendix is coauthored with Christophe Chamley.

The following assumptions were made:

(i) The DC's initial capital stock is taken equal to its steady state value K. On the other hand, the LDC is far from reaching its steady state, and

$$K_0^*/K^* - 1/3$$

(ii) $\alpha = \beta = \gamma = .3; \quad a = 1$
$\gamma = .02; \quad \lambda = .08; \quad s = .16; \quad \tau = .5$

As it turns out, the values of γ and τ are not very critical; the sum $\alpha + \beta$ may seem high but is probably reasonable if the DC's foreign investment includes human capital, or "knowledge" (the sensitivity of the solution to this assumption is examined below).

Using a gradient method, excellent convergence is obtained and table I reports the results. Table I contains a column referring to the "% of a transfer that is recouped y^*/y"; this is a straightforward application of the transfer criterion developed in chapter 2, section 2.5.

TABLE I

SIMULATION OF COMPLEMENTARITY MODEL: APPROACH TO THE STEADY STATE						
Period	K	K_F	K^*	% Of a transfer that is recouped ($y^*/y \times 100$)	θ %	Dynamic component (%)
1	6.53	1.33	.68	116.4	57	13
5	6.28	1.38	.90	113.4	57	13
10	6.25	1.46	1.11	107.7	58	12
15	6.26	1.51	1.30	102.7	58	12
20	6.30	1.57	1.45	98.3	59	11
⋮						
30	6.38	1.62	1.68	92.3	60	10
40	6.46	1.67	1.82	89.1	60	10
50	6.50	1.69	1.90	87.9	60	10
⋮						
∞ Steady State	6.50	1.73	2.00	84.6	60	10

Note that:
(i) The dynamic component is a subsidy which offsets the statically optimal tax (which equals $1 - \beta$, or 0.7). As expected from the analysis of the simplified model the optimal tax increases as the steady state level of foreign capital is reached.
(ii) Before period 15, the DC actually *gains* by giving away a unit of capital to the LDC. Even in the steady state, however, the DC recoups a substantial portion of the transfer (%).

The importance of dynamic effects in this particular model turns out to be strongly sensitive to the size of the parameters α and β. The lower are α and β (the lower the share of capital in the foreign technology) the smaller the importance of dynamic effects. If, for example, $\alpha = \beta = \gamma = 0.2$ (0.1) instead of 0.3, the % of a transfer recouped *in the steady state* is 33% (5%) instead of 85%, and the size of the dynamic component (a subsidy) is 6% instead of 10%.

Finally, we should indicate that the simulation of a model in which the DC is constrained to a steady state and the other assumptions of the special case analysed in section 3.3 are verified (i.e., linear utility and production functions) yields solutions which are qualitatively identical to solution of the general model discussed above. Moreover, the relative order of magnitude of dynamic versus static effects is the same. We speculate that the assumption that the DC is constrained to a steady state, whilst it enormously simplifies the analysis does not materially affect the results when one country is a DC and the other is a LDC.

3. Simulations were also run of a steady state model of *perfect substitution* between home and foreign capital, with the foreign production function of the form:

$$Y^* = (K^* + K_F)^\gamma$$

The following values of the parameters were assumed:
(i) The share of capital in both the home and the foreign technology were set equal to 0.3.
(ii) The propensity to save out of labor income ($S_{\bar{W}}$) and out of capital income (S_p) were allowed to range from 0 to 0.3
(iii) All other relevant parameter values were assumed equal to those of the previous section.

Table II illustrates some results; the following patterns can be discerned:

(i) The social cost of a transfer, as expected in this perfect substitution model, is always higher than its immediate cost; it varies from over twice its original cost when foreign propensities to save and the foreign capital stock are low, to about equal its original cost when they are high.

(ii) The dynamic component (which as expected becomes negative, an additional tax, when the propensity to save out of labour income is relatively high) is small compared to the total tax. The steady fall in θ which accompanies increases in the foreign propensities to save is due to the fall in the dominant static component $\left(\eta_{K_F}^r\right)$ caused by a falling proportion of the foreign capital stock which is accounted for by foreign investment.

TABLE II

SIMULATION OF PERFECT SUBSTITUTION MODEL STEADY STATE VALUES

Propensity to save in foreign country (%)					Social cost of a transfer as a percentage of immediate cost $\dfrac{y - y^*}{y} \times 100$	θ (%)	Dynamic component
Out of capital income	Out of labor income	K	K_F	K^2			
10	5	6.1	1.3	.7	206	46	1
"	10	6.0	1.2	1.4	160	34	−2
"	20	5.5	0.7	3.1	120	15	−2
20	5	6.2	1.4	1.0	195	39	2
"	10	6.0	1.2	1.9	151	27	1
"	20	5.3	0.5	3.7	111	90	0
30	5	6.3	1.5	1.3	183	32	5
"	10	5.9	1.1	2.4	139	20	0
"	20	4.9	0.2	4.5	103	0	0

---

2 Positive numbers indicate that the dynamic component is a subsidy; negative numbers that the dynamic component is an additional tax.

CHAPTER 4

The Optimal Retaliation Policy for a Small Country

4.1. INTRODUCTION

Traditionally the discussion of optimal tariffs or optimal foreign investment taxes have abstracted from the possibility of retaliation by the foreign country. In the very rare cases where this assumption has been relaxed (Johnson, 1953–4; Hamada,) the analysis of retaliation has been based on Cournot type models in which each country in turn is assumed to impose an optimal tariff or investment tax treating the foreign country's policy as given exogenously. From this assumption of "myopic" retaliation policies has stemmed at least one very interesting conclusion, that it *is* possible for one country to improve its position relative to the free trade situation even in the face of retaliation by the other country. Stated otherwise, there can exist a Cournot equilibrium (from which neither country has interest in departing) in which the country which initially began the tariff (or investment tax) "war" is better off than in the free trade situation.

An almost immediate consequence of the Cournot structure of these retaliation models is that a "small" country will always lose the tariff war, because of its inability to turn the terms of trade (or borrowing/lending) in its favour by reducing the volume of international exchange. This is easily seen in the familiar Marshall offer curve diagram of Figure 1. In this figure, L represents the large (L) country's infinitely elastic free trade offer curve, and S the offer curve of the small (S) country; the free trade equilibrium is the point A. The point B represents the first post-free trade equilibrium, after the L country has set its optimal tariff.

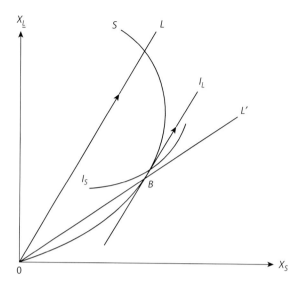

In fact, the point B is the point of tangency of the "envelope" S with the L country's indifference curve I_L, which is a straight line parallel to the offer curve L. The tariff ridden offer curve of the L country is represented by L'. The point B is clearly also the Cournot equilibrium, since country S can only lose by levying a retaliatory tariff (any new equilibrium along OB would yield a level of S country utility lower than I_L). An analogous diagram can be employed to demonstrate that a small country engaging in international investment or borrowing will inevitably lose a tax war.

The purpose of this note is to argue that, while the prediction of Cournot models that the large country will win a tariff or tax war is essentially correct, there exist a more general set of assumptions (which contain the Cournot process as a special case) under which the loss incurred by the small country due to the tariff or tax war can be much smaller than suggested by these models.

4.2. THE POSSIBILITY OF AN EXTREME THREAT

Figure 1 suggests the simple observation that, though the S country can only lower its welfare by levying a tariff given an initial equilibrium B in Figure 1, it can by its action lower the L country's welfare as well; the

S country can thus *threaten* the L country with a retaliatory tariff, and, possibly, induce the L country to adopt a more "moderate" posture. The S country can, at the limit, threaten to levy an infinitely high tariff (or tax) in retaliation to *any* tariff (or tax) that the L country may levy. This is tantamount to threatening the complete interruption of trade in the event of any attempts by the L country to exploit its monopoly position. If trade were indeed interrupted the L country would find its welfare reduced to the level of point A, the free trade equilibrium, since, as is well known,[1] a very large country's gain from trade is zero. It is clear, therefore, that barring any spiteful reactions, if the S country threatens a high enough retaliatory tariff and *if the L country believes that the threat will be carried out*, that it will be in the interest of the L country to adopt a free trade policy at the limit.

4.3. THE PROBLEM OF CREDIBILITY

The previous section has established the fairly obvious fact that a threat of "extreme" retaliation could induce the L country to adopt a close to free trade policy in its own interest. But the conclusion is subject to the proviso that the L country believes that the S country will carry out its threat, and herein lies the critical weakness of the argument, for casual empirical observation suggests that while the complete interruption of trade would in most cases cause unacceptable damage to a small country dealing with a large country or a block of countries (such as the EEC), it would cause relatively little damage to the latter. In a very real sense, then, such threats are prima facie not credible (See Schelling, Chapter 2 for a discussion of threats and credibility).

How can the S country enhance the credibility of its threats? It seems reasonable to assume that, if the S country were, for a sufficient number of "periods" (N) to consistently adopt a retaliation policy of a type γt, where $\gamma > 0$ is a reaction parameter and t is the large country's tariff (or tax), eventually the L country would come to "believe" the S country's committment, and, in its own interest, incorporate the retaliation scheme

---

[1] The reader can convince himself that L in Fig. 1 is the L country's autarky indifference curve.

into its own plans. This basic behavioural assumption will provide the cue for much of the following discussion. The reader should note that this formulation contains the atemporal Cournot adjustment scheme as a special case, corresponding to $\gamma = 0$.

Let us return for a moment to the possibility of an extreme retaliation scheme ($\gamma = \infty$). It is clear that, if we make the usual neoclassical assumptions about a decreasing marginal utility of income and a positive rate of time preference, such a policy could turn out to be prohibitively expensive, even if the S country knew for certain that after x periods the L country would finally lower its tariff[2].

4.4. THE POSSIBILITY OF A MODERATE THREAT

If extreme courses of action are unprofitable for the S country, the question naturally arises whether a more moderate threat ($\gamma < \infty$), which is actually put into practice might not be preferable to passive acceptance of the L country's trade restriction.

It is clear that in order for a moderate retaliation policy to be worthwhile two conditions have to be fulfilled: (a) the L country must find it in its interest to lower its tariff (or tax) once it incorporates the S retaliation scheme into its own decision process, (b) the resulting S country real income path (low for the first N periods, high later) must be preferable to the steady income path implied by the passive policy.

The rest of this chapter is devoted to establishing some conditions under which (a) above is verified. If (a) is verified we can presume that, for a low enough rate of time preference, a moderate retaliation policy will be preferable to a passive posture.

The investigation of the conditions under which (a) above is verified will be carried out in the context of an international investment model, preferred to the trade model because of its simpler structure.

---

2   Note that if the rate of time preference is zero and real income has constant marginal utility, then given perfect certainty and an infinite time horizon, it would always pay the S country to abstain from trade for a limited number of periods so as to reap future returns.

4.5. THE EFFECT OF THE THREAT OF RETALIATION ON THE LARGE COUNTRY'S POLICY

In what follows we consider a model where the L country invests in the S country and believes that to any L tax t the S country will respond with a tax γt, where $\gamma > 0$ is the reaction parameter. We shall derive the F.O.C. for an optimum to the L country problem and study how a change in γ affects the L country's optimal foreign investment tax.

The L country's problem can be set out as follows

$$\underset{t}{\text{Max}}\, Y_L = a(K - K_F) + r(K_F)(1 - \gamma t)K_F$$

subject to

$$a = r(K_F)(1 - \gamma t)(1 - t) \tag{1}$$

where Y_L is the L country's income; a is the rate of return to capital in the L country, constant by virtue of the assumption that L is "large"; K and K_F are the L country capital stock and foreign investment, respectively; $r(K_F)$ is the average return to foreign investment; t is the L country's tax on foreign investment.

The constraint (1) is the usual condition that the average rate or return to investment at home be equal to the average rate of return to foreign investment.

In the derivations that follow a dot over the variable will denote the derivative with respect to t, the L country tax rate $\left(\text{e.g. } \dot{K}_F = \dfrac{dK_F}{dt}\right)$.

Let Z denote the proportion of foreign investment income that is "disposable" or "net" after home and foreign taxes,

$$Z = (1 - \gamma t)(1 - t) \tag{2}$$

From (1), we obtain

$$\dot{K}_F = -\left(\dfrac{\dot{Z}}{Z}\right)\dfrac{r}{r'} \tag{1'}$$

where
$$r' = \frac{dr}{dK_F}$$

Deriving Y_L with respect to t, and using (1'), we obtain the F.O.C. for an optimum

$$a\left(\frac{\dot{Z}}{Z}\right)\frac{r}{r'} - (r'K_F + r)(1 - \gamma t)\left(\frac{\dot{Z}}{Z}\right)\frac{r}{r'} - rK_F\gamma = 0 \quad (3)$$

Using condition (1) above, and dividing through by rK_F, (3) can be written

$$\frac{\dot{Z}}{\frac{r'K_F}{r}} - \frac{\dot{Z}}{Z}\left(\frac{1}{\frac{r'K_F}{r}}\right)\left(\frac{r'K_F}{r} + 1\right)(1 - \gamma t) - \gamma = 0 \quad (3')$$

Defining
$$\beta = \frac{-r'K_F}{r}$$

the elasticity of the rate of return of foreign investment with respect to foreign investment, and multiplying through by βZ, we can rewrite (3')

$$-\dot{Z}Z + \dot{Z}(1 - \beta)(1 - rt) - \gamma Z\beta = 0. \quad (3'')$$

Next, note that
$$\dot{Z} = 2\gamma t - 1 - \gamma$$

and let, for convenience,
$$\eta = 1 - \beta.$$

Using these relations, and the definition of Z, and collecting coefficients of the same power (3'') can be written

$$(2\gamma^2)t^3 + (\gamma^3\eta - 2\gamma^2 - 3\gamma)t^2 + (1 - 2\gamma\eta + 3\gamma)t + (\eta - 1) = (\quad (3''')$$

The optimal foreign investment tax rate for the large country is given by one (or more) of the three roots of a third-degree polynomial.

We can see immediately from (3''') that $\gamma = 0$ implies $t = 1 - \eta = \beta$, the optimal tax rate in the absence of retaliation, underlining the fact that our retaliation model contains the Cournot model as a special case.

Condition (3''') can be differentiated totally to identify the effect of a change in the S country's reaction parameter on the level of the L country's foreign investment tax.

Differentiating equation (3''') with respect to t and γ, we have

$$d\gamma(4\gamma t^3 + (2\gamma\eta + \gamma^2\eta_\gamma - 4\gamma - 3)t^2 + (-2\eta + 3 - 2\gamma\eta_\gamma)t + \eta_\gamma) + dt(3t^2(2\gamma^2) + 2t(\gamma^2\eta - 2\gamma^2 - 3\gamma) + \eta_t\gamma^2 t^2 + (1 - 2\gamma n + 3\gamma) - 2\gamma t\eta_t + \eta_t) = 0 \qquad (4)$$

Unfortunately, it does not appear possible to make any general statement about the sign of the coefficients of $d\gamma$ and dt in (4). We can, however, obtain the following interesting result: *if the elasticity of the foreign rate of return with respect to foreign investment (γ) is constant, and if we depart from a situation where the S country does not threaten retaliation (i.e. $\gamma = 0$), then a "moderate" threat of retaliation will induce the L country to lower its tax rate.*

To see this, note that setting in equation (4) above $\gamma = \eta_\gamma = \eta_t = 0$ we obtain

$$\frac{dt}{d\gamma} = 3t^2 - 3t = 3t(t-1) < 0 \qquad (5)$$

Thus, given that η is constant (or approximately constant), the S country can induce the L country to lower its tax rate by threatening a "small" retaliatory tax, and condition (a) of the previous section is fulfilled.

This result demonstrates that in a constant elasticity model condition (a) of the previous section is fulfilled provided we depart from a situation where the S country is passive. Below, we shall present the results of some computer simulations which indicate that in the constant elasticity model, condition (a) is in fact fulfilled regardless of the S country's initial posture with regard to retaliation. Before this is done, however, we need to consider the issue of the S country's behaviour *after* the L country has "believed" the S country's threat and lowered its tax.

Specifically, should the S country revert to a free trade policy after the large country lowers its tax? It can be argued that in order to maintain the credibility of its retaliatory policy (i.e., to set a tax equal to γt always) that the S country *must* implement the tax as threatened for otherwise the L country may revert to old habits. Assuming the S country carries out the threat the question naturally arises whether the S country actually benefits from its retaliatory policy.

It is important to realise that (5) by itself does not ensure that the real income of the S country will rise relative to its level under a passive policy. For when the threat is carried out, foreign investment is clearly reduced, and this cost has to be weighed against the benefit of a lower foreign tax rate. Clearly, a sufficient condition for the S country income to increase relative to its level under a passive policy is that Z, the proportion of foreign investment income left over after L and S taxes, increases with the threat of retaliation, since this automatically implies an expanded foreign investment.

We shall now show that, assuming we depart from a situation where $\gamma = 0$, that S country income does in fact rise. To see this, derive condition (2) with respect to γ to obtain

$$\frac{\partial Z}{\partial \gamma} = 3t(1-t) - t + t^2 \qquad (6)$$

or

$$\frac{\partial Z}{\partial \gamma} = 2t(1-t) > 0$$

completing the proof of the following proposition

> *If η is constant, and the S country's threat is both believed and carried out a little retaliation is better than no retaliation.*

The question naturally arises whether given a constant η the above result can be extended to cases where initially $\gamma > 0$. Unfortunately, demonstration of this proposition requires the use of condition (4) together with the use of the second order conditions, and these proved to be too intricate to yield an unambiguous result. The stratagem adopted has been to investigate the solution for equation (3′′′) under various assumptions using an electronic computer. The roots to the equation (3′′′) were found using the standard formula for the roots of a third-degree polynomial. For all values of the parameters assumed all roots of the polynomial were found to be real. The selected root (tax) is the one which implies the highest L country income, given by

$$Y_L = a(K - K_F) + \eta K^{*\alpha} K_F^{\eta}(1 - \gamma t)$$

where K^* is the S country's capital stock.

We note the following:

For all values of the parameters assumed, the computer solution yields a level of S country real income which increases with γ. Also, t always decreases when γ increases.

We should emphasise that in quantifying the change in S country income we have assumed throughout that the S country remains faithful to its retaliation scheme even *after* the L country lowers its tax rate.

The results of a typical simulation are reported in table 1, where the following parameter assumptions were made

$$a = 0.1, \quad \eta = 0.4, \quad K^* = 1$$

In table 1, Y_S represents the small country's level of income and ΔY_L represents the change in the large country's income with respect to the free trade situation.

Note that since $\eta = 0.4$, the no-retaliation optimal tax is 0.6.

Simulation of the model for values of η equal to 0.2, 0.6, 0.8 yielded analogous results.

| \multicolumn{5}{c}{RESULTS FROM THE SIMULATION OF THE RETALIATION MODEL} |
γ	t	ΔY_L	Y_S	K_F
0.1	.57	.3	.85	2.2
0.2	.54	.27	.89	2.24
0.3	.51	.24	.93	2.31
0.4	.48	.22	.96	2.4
0.5	.44	.2	1	2.52
0.6	.41	.18	1.03	2.63
0.7	.38	.17	1.06	2.75
0.8				
0.9				
1				
1.1				
1.2	.26	.11	1.16	3.24
⋮				
2.2	.16	.07	1.25	3.75
⋮				
3.2				
⋮				
4.2				
⋮				
5.2				
⋮				
6.2	.06	.03	1.33	4.27

4.6. SUMMARY AND CONCLUSIONS

Our principal result can be restated as follows. Assuming that (a) the L country "believes" the S country's retaliation policy after a finite number of periods where the S country carries out its threat, and the L country incorporates the threat in its decision process and (b) the elasticity of the rate of return with respect to foreign investment is constant, we have shown that it can be in the interest of the small country to retaliate even if it has to carry out the threat and that (probably) the more extreme the threat, the higher the potential (future) gains.

Do the results of Table 1 necessarily suggest that it is in the interest of the S country to threaten "extreme" retaliation? On the basis of the discussion in section 3 of this chapter, clearly not, since extreme retaliation policies may involve unacceptable short run losses. The optimal retaliation policy can be found only after definition of an explicit long run welfare functional, as well as definition of the number of periods required to "convince" the L country.

REFERENCES

Hamada, K., "Strategic Aspects of Taxation on Foreign Investment Income", *Quarterly Journal of Economics*, August 1966.

Johnson, H. G., "Optimum Tariffs and Retaliation", *The Review of Economic Studies*, 1953–54.

Schelling, T. C., *The Strategy of Conflict*, Oxford University Press, 1960.

ACKNOWLEDGEMENTS

This book is my Ph.D. Dissertation completed at the Harvard Economics Department in 1977. Publication after 45 years calls for an explanation. On completing the dissertation, I was strongly encouraged by my advisor to submit two articles based on it (Chapters 2 and 3) in one of the top journals. But by the time I finished, I had already opted for a career in business, and could not devote the time even if I had wanted to. Having returned to academic pursuits quite recently, I reviewed the relevant literature and concluded that the results I obtained back in 1977 remain new (uncovered) and important to rationalizing foreign aid, trade preferences, etc.

My greatest debt in writing the dissertation (and ever since) is to my wife Gilda who was mainly responsible for the decision to resume my studies and complete the dissertation; she also supported the family during my research, and even typed the preliminary version of the dissertation.

Professor Hendrik Houthakker, Chairman of the Thesis Committee, was in many ways the ideal thesis adviser. From the beginning he took a very active interest in the central questions of the dissertation. He made many suggestions relating to the construction of the various models and offered badly needed advice at the strategic junctures without ever attempting to impose his point of view. His ability to immediately focus on the crucial issue of a problem was of invaluable help. He was also very helpful with personal matters when the need arose.

Professor Jerry Green read the entire manuscript and made several useful comments, especially relating to the analysis of stability.

My friend and fellow graduate student Christophe Chamley contributed his admirable skills in economic theory, mathematics and computer programming to the Appendix of Chapter 3 (which is coauthored). He also helped make life humorous.

So did my friend Laurence Kotlikoff who also made perceptive suggestions on an early draft.

I would also like to acknowledge the contribution of Professor John Lintner, Chairman of the Business Economics Committee who provided advice throughout my studies at Harvard, and who allotted the computer time necessary to complete my research.

Finally, I would like to thank Kate Crowley for having typed the original manuscript in such excellent fashion.